KU-712-958

THE MACMILLAN SHAKESPEARE

GENERAL EDITOR: PETER HOLLINDALE

Senior Lecturer in English and Education,
University of York

ADVISORY EDITOR: PHILIP BROCKBANK

Professor of English and Director of
the Shakespeare Institute, University of Birmingham

TWELFTH NIGHT

OR

WHAT YOU WILL

Other titles in the series:

THE MACMILLAN SHAKESPEARE

TWELFTH NIGHT

OR

WHAT YOU WILL

Edited by

E. A. J. Honigmann

M

Macmillan Education

First published 1972
Reprinted 1973, 1977 (twice), 1978, 1979
1981 (twice)

Published by
MACMILLAN EDUCATION LTD
Houndmills Basingstoke Hampshire RG21 2XS
and London
Associated companies in Delhi Dublin
Hong Kong Johannesburg Lagos Melbourne
New York Singapore and Tokyo

Printed in Hong Kong

CONTENTS

INTRODUCTION

Samuel Pepys, the diarist, an enthusiastic theatregoer, saw *Twelfth Night* at least three times, and became more depressed with each visit: after the third, in 1669, he lamented that he had been to 'one of the weakest plays that I ever saw on the stage'.

Three hundred years later we take a very different view. Theatre audiences and professional critics admire *Twelfth Night* as Shakespeare's finest comedy, even after comparing it with masterpieces such as *A Midsummer Night's Dream* and *As You Like It* and *The Tempest*. Yet, despite this agreement, modern interpretations of the play differ quite extraordinarily, reading it as happy comedy, sad comedy, dark comedy, or near tragedy. In the theatre the comedy is sometimes reduced to the level of farce, with a Malvolio hobbled and tripped by his own garters, a Viola who actually duels with Sir Andrew (for which the text gives no excuse); or the story is extravagantly sentimentalised, 'drowning the production', it has been said, 'in golden light and drifting rose leaves'.

The critics disagree about the correct label for *Twelfth Night* because, like Feste's *opal*, it perpetually changes its colour, or mood: at one moment boisterous, then poetical, or high-fantastical, or sad, or serious. These moods, far from being disconnected, shade off into one another and interact, creating a distinctive tone for the whole play, dark for one man, lighter for another, according to their response to details. Before discussing the tone, or nature of the play, it will therefore be best to examine some of the disputed details – which can be done most conveniently by glancing at different interpretations of some of the characters.

Olivia   To take a simple but crucial case first – Olivia's age. We have to consider two conflicting theories, one of which sees her as almost a child, the other as much older. It will be self-evident that an audience's response to

1

Olivia (and, indirectly, to the whole play, since she knits together so many of its threads) must be affected by her age. Sweet sixteen may fall head-over-heels in love, and throw herself at the first pretty boy that comes along, without arousing too much satirical laughter; sweet thirty-six is not so privileged, not, at least, in the golden world of literary romance. Many producers, perhaps out of a mistaken notion that comedy means laughter, prefer a mature Olivia; and there are also editors who defend her.

> It has somewhere been suggested that the stage-tradition which presents her as a staid *châtelaine* – a *femme de trente ans* or so – is a mistake; that her swift barter of mourning for love, and of one love at a moment's notice, for another, better befits an irresponsible girl. . . . It may be so; but acquaintance with matronly ladies and the strength of their impulses may incline us to reflect that the stage-tradition is not so wrong after all.

The other side calls for an Olivia 'pretty and young as a rose-bud'.

> For far too long, more than mature leading ladies have confronted us with the not very delectable prospect of solid worth extended in corsetted melancholy upon some comfortless *chaise-longue*, distressingly besotted on a girl-boy and finally marrying the latter's twin-brother. Could anything be less Illyrian?

Both popular extremes, the rose-bud and the staid *châtelaine*, must, I fear, be rejected. Rebuking the formidable Malvolio or putting an over-insistent duke in his place, Olivia plays the great lady effortlessly – for her the rôle is not a new one. But that is not to say that she is a solid matron. We must rest content with a compromise, an Olivia exactly in her prime – how can we dispute this when Viola concedes it so grudgingly?

> 'Tis beauty truly blent, whose red and white
> Nature's own sweet and cunning hand laid on.

$$\text{(I. 5. 242–3)}$$

I have mentioned the rose-bud and the staid *châtelaine* because they illustrate two ways in which *Twelfth Night* can be misread. The twin dangers are a sentimentalised Olivia (and play), or an Olivia (and play) degraded to the level of farce. True, Olivia's unrequited passion for Cesario is closely related to Malvolio's for herself, and might therefore be thought to deserve the same derision – but Shakespeare took care, when a character was so delicately balanced, to guide his audience's response through the response of other characters. The others jeer at Malvolio, gloat over him, treat him as a madman. No one even smiles at Olivia, no one enjoys her love-pains – on the contrary, Viola defines the correct response as pity: 'Poor lady, she were better love a dream' (II. 2. 26), 'I pity you' (III. 1. 127).

We too should pity Olivia rather than laugh at her – pity her with an inward smile, for of course one cannot deny that her situation is also comical. The dramatist precludes a *predominantly* amused response by, first of all, suggesting through Viola, whom we trust, that pity is more appropriate, and secondly, by allowing Olivia to see the ridiculousness of her loving someone as hostile as Cesario. Olivia thus differs from Malvolio, a truly ridiculous lover, in her self-knowledge.

Whilst we watch Olivia's growing infatuation we remain half-conscious of the 'sentimental' romance setting and of the 'farcical' implications. As Shakespeare dwells upon her helplessness and torment, however, the presentation becomes increasingly serious – so that when she exposes herself to Cesario, knowing that she may be scorned, she speaks quietly, painfully. In short, Olivia's predicament can engage us at the human level, though never completely. It is important to recognise that comedy may allow apparently irreconcilable responses to interplay – amusement, pity, sympathy – because in *Twelfth Night* Shakespeare exploits the 'divided response' through so many characters.

Viola Even more than Olivia, Viola has suffered from the sentimentalists. They think of her as a maiden pure, *sans peur et sans reproche*, and they worship her tenderly passive nature. Viola, said one,

> simply allows herself to be carried along by the stream of time and events, which answer to her confidence by floating her at last to happiness. . . . The loss of a brother rests on her heart as on Olivia's, and she has not yet recovered courage to attempt to steer her fate.

This interpretation rests upon Viola's concluding words in Act II scene 2 ('O time, thou must untangle this, not I'), and upon the common belief that in her great love-scene with Orsino she speaks of herself when she describes her 'sister'.

> She never told her love,
> But let concealment, like a worm i' the bud,
> Feed on her damask cheek. She pined in thought . . .
> (II. 4. 110–12)

According to an eye-witness, the actress Ellen Terry played Viola's 'sister' speeches differently.

> It is not very seriously of herself that she tells the story about concealment feeding on the damask cheek . . . Viola is hearty, though not heart-whole, and Miss Terry persuades us readily that the true Viola is one from whose gentle nature gaiety is not likely to be permanently estranged.

The love-scene itself can be viewed in two entirely different ways. If we believe in a passive Viola we may suppose that as she comes close, again and again, to revealing her secret to the unsuspecting Orsino, she surrenders to the temptation of the moment, the wish to be known for what she is – in short, that her tender feelings overwhelm all other considerations, until Orsino's impercipience brings her down to earth again. On the other hand, since Viola has already proved brilliantly adroit in repartee and

4

quick-witted in emergency, in her interviews with Olivia and Malvolio, we may reasonably imagine her as having the same character in her love-scene – which would mean that, instead of very nearly betraying herself against her will, she cleverly drops hints in order to open Orsino's eyes. Speaking of her 'sister' she can *act* the sister, sitting down in a posture reminiscent of 'Patience on a monument', and 'smiling at grief', in the hope that all her hints that she is a 'lady' will click into place. Her last and most undisguised hint, 'I am all the daughters of my father's house', is not easy to explain except on some such hypothesis.

Before we choose between the two Violas it will be useful to glance at the story as Shakespeare found it in his 'source', a *novella* by Barnaby Rich. Here the original Viola fell in love with the original Orsino while he stayed briefly at her father's palace, and, when he sailed away, quite unaware of her passion, she sailed after him, suffered shipwreck, survived it, disguised herself as a boy, and proceeded to Orsino's court. (The rest of the story is not relevant to our immediate purposes – Orsino's love-suit to Olivia, Viola's being sent as his messenger, the arrival of Sebastian and the double marriage at the end are more or less as in Shakespeare, except that he changed all the names.)

Rather than the traditional passively-tender Viola, Shakespeare could have intended one not too unlike her original, one that pursues her man with remorseless efficiency, the kind of woman of whom Bernard Shaw said – 'You might as well refuse to accept the embraces of a boa constrictor when once she gets round your neck.' It all depends on the speaking of one line. 'Orsino?' she says (I. 2. 26), 'I have heard my father name him.' If Viola was then instructed to catch her breath, or to betray a special concern as she goes on 'He was . . . *a bachelor then*' (a question begging for information if there ever was one), an audience cannot fail to suspect what Barnaby Rich spelt out so explicitly, that Viola has come to get her man.

The significant thing about the two interpretations of Viola is that neither can be proved. Shakespeare offers us 'impressions' of his heroine, which are rapidly overlaid by other impressions, even conflicting ones, thus building in our minds an intuition of character that is vivid in some respects and confused in others – very much like our understanding of real people. When we hear 'he was a bachelor then' we are alerted; when, two scenes later, after only three days at Orsino's court, Viola sighs 'Whoe'er I woo, myself would be his wife', we may wonder about their earlier acquaintance – for which Sebastian, two scenes later again, adduces further clues when he declares himself 'bound to the Count Orsino's court' (suggesting that Viola, in the same ship, was on her way there as well, as in Rich's *novella*). But the mystery is never solved. Orsino may be no more than a name to Viola in Act I, scene 2, she may thereupon fall in love at first sight, and Sebastian may go to Orsino's court only because a shipwreck has cast him up in Illyria. Similarly, in the love-scene, Shakespeare chose to give us conflicting impressions: Viola seems the passive maiden, seems to give herself away in unreflecting tenderness, and at the same time she seems perfectly in control of the situation and always a move or two ahead of Orsino.

The style of Viola's celebrated love-speech (II. 4. 110–15) reinforces her ambivalence. Heightened poetic language suggests genuine emotion, and yet we cannot rid ourselves of the suspicion that Viola perhaps switches into what is almost poetical attitudinising in order to compete with Orsino's earlier extravagance (II. 4. 93–113). He challenged her with his greater passion, and she takes up the challenge. Or is it that she simply responds to his passion? The image, barely avoided, of a green and yellow 'Patience on a monument', shows how delicately Shakespeare balanced laughter and pathos – or rather, concealed the one within the other, 'like a worm i' th' bud'.

6

One can only conclude that Shakespeare imagined Viola as both dazzlingly clever and tenderly passionate – if you like, a feminine Hamlet – and that, as in the case of Hamlet, he preferred not to explain precisely how her mind worked. We accept this because we know that Hamlet, when he fails to kill the kneeling Claudius, and Viola, when she speaks so oddly to Orsino in the love-scene, are both under tremendous pressure, and therefore we don't expect completely normal behaviour.

Orsino In her exchanges with Olivia and Maria and Toby, Viola's cleverness glitters in all that she says, whilst at Orsino's court it seems to operate beneath the verbal surface – here she does not display her wit as a peacock displays his tail. The reason may be that Orsino's self-indulgent passion could not stand comparison with a keen intelligence without impressing us as mere witlessness, and that Viola's brightness was accordingly dimmed. For, though opinions differ, it is probably wrong to take Orsino as a satiric portrait. In his very first scene he may strike us as a Moony Duke, but as he succumbs to Viola's magic, and drops some of his posturing, and speaks more naturally ('Dear lad, believe it', 'But died thy sister of her love, my boy?'), his true character reveals itself and proves more worthy of her. Deep answers unto deep: he has a generous nature, like Viola, quick to sympathise with others, artistic, and essentially humble. Whether he ever becomes entirely worthy of her is, however, another question.

Malvolio Of all the characters in *Twelfth Night*, Malvolio has provoked the sharpest disagreement. Do we sympathise with him as the victim of an outrageous plot, or do we merely dislike him and enjoy his discomfiture? Do we respond to him as human, or as farcically grotesque? The alternatives can be illustrated from two famous productions. Beerbohm Tree, in 1901, decided on a grotesque steward and briskly heightened Malvolio for the theatre: an intolerably condescending blue-eyed peacock with a red twirl of beard and a quizzing-glass, a man spanieled by four minor Malvolios, the images of their master, who stiffened to attention behind him when he spoke.

In Granville-Barker's production of 1912 Malvolio struck the reviewers as brilliantly subdued.

His reproof of the roisterers at their midnight orgy is that of his mistress's faithful servant, shocked on *her* account, rather than that of a tyrant, outraged on his own.

There is little that is fantastic about [this] Malvolio, whose dress and demeanor are sombre, whose movements are few and simple, whose discourse is studied, but spoken very quietly.[1]

Those who insist on Malvolio's humanity owe much to an essay, first published in 1822, in which Charles Lamb described how a once-popular actor, Robert Bensley, played the part. Bensley made one believe in Malvolio as a 'sensible and spirited' human being, with genuine 'dignity'.

He was starch, spruce, opinionated, but his superstructure of pride seemed bottomed upon a sense of worth. There was something in it beyond the coxcomb . . . I confess that I never saw the catastrophe of this character, while Bensley played it, without a kind of tragic interest.

An ingenious essay recently tried to explain away Bensley's Malvolio as, almost, one of Lamb's 'dream children', since Lamb, only twenty-one when Bensley retired from the stage, wrote his essay about him a quarter of a century later, from memory. But what does this prove? If Lamb, and not Bensley, was the first to pro-

[1] *The Times* and *The Morning Post*, 1912.

claim a 'tragic interest' in Malvolio we cannot disallow Lamb's Malvolio as a late critical aberration, since next to nothing is recorded about the playing of the part before Bensley. For all we know the very first Malvolio could have been exactly as Lamb described him. But we don't know, and therefore all that matters is that subsequent theatrical experience confirms the legitimacy of Lamb's perception.

Of the many good reasons against reducing Malvolio to the level of a mere comic butt let us restrict ourselves to a single one – that our sympathies remain too confused to permit of such simple classification. The 'comic butt' advocates claim that 'our sympathies are all with Malvolio's foes'. One must retort that Olivia and Viola don't sympathise with Malvolio's foes, so why should we? We are torn in different directions in different scenes, as in all of Shakespeare's best plays.

Shakespeare, it should be noticed, brought the argument into the story. On behalf of the roisterers Fabian urges that their plot should 'pluck on laughter' (V. 1. 368), and not be taken too seriously. Malvolio, however, insists on its seriousness, and threatens revenge. When Olivia delivers judgment one word used by her carries a special weight, since Malvolio had previously appropriated it: 'Fool, there was never man so *notoriously* abused' (IV. 2. 90); 'Madam, you have done me wrong,/*Notorious* wrong' (V. 1. 330); '[You have made me] the most *notorious* geck and gull' (V. 1. 345). Which position does Olivia adopt? 'He hath been most *notoriously* abused' – Malvolio's, not Fabian's. So it seems, though she may just possibly speak with laughter in her voice, contradicting her own words. Yet the fact that Shakespeare makes the two attitudes compete for our approval more or less simultaneously, that they may even fuse in Olivia's summing-up, and the fact that critics respond to both, suggests that here, and in earlier episodes, a 'divided response' would be not unnatural. It will incline more towards laughter in the box-tree scene, and more towards pity at the close, without the one ever completely displacing the other.

Feste the Jester has been called the 'master-mind and controller of *Twelfth Night*, its comic spirit and president'. If the character who most closely approximates to a chorus is misunderstood, how can we hope to do justice to the play? A. C. Bradley, probably the most influential of twentieth-century Shakespeare critics, admired the 'serenity and gaiety' of Feste's spirit, and thought of the jester as living in a 'sunny realm of flitting fancies'.

> This sunshine of the breast is always with him, and spreads its radiance over the whole scene in which he moves. And so we love him.[1]

True – or not true? Feste's nature, according to Bradley, expresses itself unmistakably in his songs, 'Come away, come away, death', 'O mistress mine', 'When that I was'. It may be so; but the *quality* of Feste's music, and of his temperament, emerges more significantly from the closing than from the opening lines of his songs: 'Youth's a stuff will not endure', 'For the rain it raineth every day'. The last in particular, the refrain of a song sung entirely for his own pleasure, unbidden, after the principals have left the stage, gives the essence of Feste – a wryly-smiling, open-eyed, undefeated acceptance of life, cheerful where the occasion demands it but otherwise too *knowing* to deceive himself.

'Happiness', said Swift, 'is a perpetual possession of being well deceived.' An exaggeration, yet we have to admit that there is a qualitative difference between a happy and a thoughtful mind. In Feste's case I am impressed above all by his sly penetration, his cheerfulness strikes me as professional rather than temperamental, and the effect is then far from sunny.

Bradley also commented on Feste's shameless begging[2],

[1] 'Feste the Jester' in *A Miscellany*, 1929.
[2] See III. 1. 51–5, V. 1. 27–48.

which he explained as resulting from a fool's economic dependence and uncertainty about the future; and he thought that Feste's failure to 'make a third' in the plot against Malvolio[1] had a similar motive, that is, the dependent fool had 'to keep clear of any really dangerous enterprise'. The way in which Feste squares up to Malvolio at the end of the play quite contradicts this view, however, for Malvolio does not know, and might never have known, about Feste's part as Sir Topas: Feste tells him, as provokingly as possible, twisting the knife until Malvolio can no longer bear it.

I object to a Feste who will not take risks because I do not see him, at the end of the play, as a cautious opportunist who kicks Malvolio when he is down, and, more importantly, because Feste's inner strength, his intellectual independence, is so unmistakably present in one's overall impression of the man. Bradley saw Feste's shameless begging as simply an *economic* necessity, while Shakespeare seems to have probed more deeply. Feste takes toll of those who, in Bertie Wooster's phrase, are 'rolling in the stuff', with, almost invariably, expressions of independence, even of contempt. It is a *psychological* necessity – to expose himself to patronage and, hey presto, to turn the tables and patronise the giver, for he can thus reassure himself of the inferiority of his social betters. His most flagrant gesture of this kind was his not bothering to thank Sir Andrew for a handsome present of sixpence. (It cost only *one* penny to see *Twelfth Night* at the Globe theatre.) Reminded by Sir Andrew, he replies 'I did impeticos thy gratillity'. Learned editors tell us that this is nonsense: it remains to point out that here, as elsewhere, Feste proves incapable of saying 'thank you' pleasantly.

As intriguing as his coolness when he receives money, and as clear a sign of his independence, are Feste's absences from Olivia's home. The first fact we learn about him, usually a significant fact in Shakespeare, is that he

[1] See II. 3. 180, and p. 24.

will have to explain a lengthy absence (I. 5. 1). Where has he been? To understand we have only to listen to his songs, preoccupied as they are with unfulfilled or thwarted love – 'O mistress mine, where are you roaming?' In 'Come away, come away, death' the mistress behaves unkindly again ('I am slain by a fair, cruel maid'), and Feste's final song also gives us the disappointed lover ('But when I came, alas, to wive').

Some say that Feste, the complete professional, chooses his songs to suit the mood of his listeners – that the songs tell us nothing about the singer. Have they looked at the context? Of the three principal songs, the last, 'When that I was', has no stage-listeners at all; after the second, 'Come away, come away, death', Feste explains, after Orsino has apologised for asking for a painful love-song, that he enjoyed singing it. As for the first, 'O mistress mine', he offers an alternative – 'Would you have a love-song, or a song of good life?' But what kind of alternative was that? Feste rightly anticipates that his audience (Toby and Andrew) 'care not for good life', and in effect he offers them a choice of one out of one.

I now come to Bradley's boldest assertion. 'We never laugh at Feste. He would not dream of marrying Audrey.' (Touchstone, the fool in *As You Like It*, marries Audrey.) On the contrary, there are signs that Feste dreams all through *Twelfth Night* of a fair, cruel maid. First, his songs. Next, Sir Andrew knows he has a sweetheart, and sent her sixpence (II. 3. 25). Then, Feste's absences. Maria's prying questions, in Feste's first scene (I. 5), are silenced by his remark that 'if Sir Toby would leave drinking, thou wert as witty a piece of Eve's flesh as any in Illyria' (as if to say 'I know a thing or two about Toby and you, and about *your* love-life'). This suggests that she was prying into *his* love-life – that she suspected him of having been away with his sweetheart. He seems, even, to admit as much, in the line 'Many a good hanging prevents a bad marriage' (i.e. 'if I were well hung I would escape this bad marriage')[1]. These hints are too scattered to *disprove* Bradley's assertion, but they offer an alternative. Instead of a Feste sunnily serene, and immune to pang of heart, we may substitute one who is wryly mournful, who puts on gaiety as a mask.

Sir Toby Belch   Technically, Belch has the rôle of the villain of *Twelfth Night*, in so far as he intrigues against others for his own ends. The technical villain may of course strike us as the most likeable person in the play – for example, Cassius in *Julius Caesar* – and therefore we must ask ourselves precisely what pleasure, if any, we take in Belch.

Sentimentalists, who prefer to call him Sir Toby, describe him as 'the spirit of Merrie England', 'good-natured Toby', and Quiller-Couch went so far as to adapt a saying of Burke – that in Toby 'vice has lost half its evil by losing all its grossness'. Against this it has been pertinently urged that 'with Sir Toby's first belch, revelry as a way of life seems somehow less appealing'. One might add that in different productions Sir Toby can be heard to belch in very different decibels – decorously, even elegantly, or naturalistically, and, not quite so often, with an awesome thunderous percussion. His grossness, in short, can be softened or accentuated. Producers with a weakness for pretty dresses and golden light tend to tone it down, quite forgetting that 'Belch' is an authorial stage-direction overriding all critical theories about the play's poignancy, sweetness, cleanness, delicacy. To deny Sir Toby his belch, and his other natural explosions, is to emasculate a play that can be all too easily prettified and stripped of Shakespeare's characteristic comical sharpness.

In itself, Toby's grossness gives no offence, except to the most squeamish. But it should be observed that he

[1] Some editors believe that this line refers to Maria's hope of marrying Sir Toby, but the context makes it apply more naturally to Feste. The implications here (I. 5. 1–30) are none too clear, except that Feste and Maria spar for an advantage.

uses it as a screen to hide a less pleasant side of himself. One way or another we are reminded throughout the play that he is bleeding Sir Andrew white – his gross camaraderie serves as the predator's camouflage. 'I have been dear to him, lad, some two thousand strong or so' (III. 2. 54–5). The speech about Sir Andrew's hair ('It hangs like flax on a distaff; and I hope to see a huswife take thee between her legs and spin it off', I. 3. 103–5) describes his *own* relationship to his dear manikin; he has him in a vice-like grip, and spins off his money. The grim humour of it, and the fanciful image, half-conceals Toby's relentless selfishness, which is elsewhere eased out of the picture by raucous laughter, hiccups and belching.

Toby's defenders sometimes insist that those who do not love him have given way to modern (i.e. unhistorical and therefore false) attitudes. Though Toby drives Malvolio close to desperation, and behaves disgracefully in Olivia's house, and swindles Sir Andrew, they say that the Elizabethans warmed to all practical jokes and revelry, and would have delighted in Toby. The same critics assure us, baldly, that 'our sympathies are all with Malvolio's foes'. A moment's thought should suffice to show that Shakespeare is not so straightforward. If we are to sympathise with Toby's revelry, why is he dismissed at the end with a broken head? Olivia, when she has heard Toby's case and Malvolio's, condemns Toby, and appears to 'sum up' for the dramatist (V. 1. 347). I suggest that, all things considered, our response to Toby should be one of severely chastened rapture. He is, at times, very funny, yet it is possible that we repudiate him even as we laugh with him, and that in the box-tree scene we find him almost as outrageous as Malvolio. After all, Sir Andrew laughs at Malvolio too, but we do not sympathise, or identify ourselves, with him.

The Underplot Feste, Toby and Maria, the moving spirits of the underplot, have more in common than their love of laughter. Without making too much of it, Shake-speare indicates that they all live in economic dependence – and don't like it. Feste has to take tips, and resents the necessity; Toby knows that the evil day will come when 'there shall be no more cakes and ale'; and Maria escapes from service into a far from ideal marriage. All three joke, and laugh, and put on a show, yet the general impression is not simply one of Merrie England, for money passes from hand to hand and the rogues use jollity as a cover. We never quite forget that Toby is milking Sir Andrew, that Maria torments Malvolio partly to entangle Toby in marriage, and that Feste humours the knights who call him *sot* in order to pick up sixpences. Through the haze of good cheer we should see, in Chaucer's immortal phrase, 'the smiler with the knife under the cloak'. The underplot thus contributes not merely a frolic, not merely sunny radiance and good-nature, but a sense of the precarious-ness of life, reinforcing the main plot's poetical suggestion of life's fragility.

The 'Happy Ending' It will now be clear that the non-comic aspects of *Twelfth Night* deserve special attention. To discuss in isolation the 'tragedy' of Malvolio or the mournfulness of Feste or the sharpness of Toby is to miss an important cumulative effect. We must recognise that all of the play's potentially painful moments reinforce one another, while remembering that they may be painful and yet, in a limited sense, comical – just as there may be a residual comical incongruity in moments of high tragedy, such as King Lear's crazy trial of his daughters in the storm-scene. Orsino seems in pain, real or imagined, throughout the play; Malvolio suffers in the dark room, and in the final scene, and Olivia's rebuke, 'O, you are sick of self-love, Malvolio' (I. 5. 91), may go through him like a knife; Feste must hate Malvolio's 'barren rascal' sneer (I. 5. 84), or he would not cast it up against him five acts later; above all, Viola and Olivia, as they both confess, are driven to frenzy and desperation by their love.

If the major and secondary characters are, to adapt a line from *Tam o'Shanter*, 'nursing their pain to keep it warm', the final scene can become a powerful dramatic crescendo. Though the double marriage at the end has been identified with the 'happy ending' of altar-trotting in romance, we should notice that the two pairs of lovers consciously enter a love-relationship with their partners only in the closing moments of the play. In Shakespeare's 'happy comedies' the romantic lover and his lass usually know each other for what they are, whereas Orsino, Olivia and Sebastian marry in ignorance – and we are bound to wonder what will come of it. Shakespeare's 'dark comedies', it should be added, throw together the principals as suddenly, and leave us at the end with the same question.

It is often taken for granted that Olivia is a lucky lady in her 'happy union' with Sebastian. Does she herself give that impression? Human nature surely rebels against the thought of marriage to a total stranger – and the characters of *Twelfth Night* are sufficiently complex to interest us as human beings, as distinct from the pasteboard figures of conventionalised romance. In Elizabethan comedy the discovery that one had married the wrong person was, indeed, a not uncommon punishment, never a happy ending. I am not suggesting that Olivia deserves punishment, only that we should place the natural interpretation upon her not speaking to Sebastian – that she is uncomfortable. Theirs may well turn into a happy union later, yet the note upon which Shakespeare chose to dismiss them from *Twelfth Night* was different. Similarly, we are disturbed by Orsino's last line, his description of Viola as 'Orsino's mistress and his *fancy's* queen', an ominous reminder of his *fancy's* fickleness (compare I. 1. 14–15, II. 4. 33–6).

To return to the drama and pain of the last scene, let us list some of the details. Viola is accused of ingratitude by Antonio, of base fear by Olivia, and of dissembling by

Orsino. Poor Olivia publicly shames herself in claiming a husband who shrinks from her. Orsino, in anguish, threatens to kill Olivia and Viola; Sir Andrew and Sir Toby enter hurt, with broken heads; the madly-used Malvolio rages against his tormentors. Much of this can be stylised and toned down – so that Viola's distress, when all turn against her, becomes merely a pretty confusion, Orsino's fury a passing whim, and even the broken heads could be carried off with bravura. On the other hand, the text allows us to imagine that Andrew and Toby have been so badly mauled that one gasps to see them; that Olivia bursts into tears with her line 'Ay me detested, how am I beguiled!' And if Orsino strikes Viola heavily across the face, which has been done in the theatre, as they slowly recoil and look into each other's eyes, horror-stricken after the blow, their strange relationship can suddenly explode – here, in what may be the play's most poignant moment, though there is no positive stage direction for it, it could dawn on him at last that he loves Cesario. Physical violence and genuine grief must have a part in the final scene, I think, because the whole comedy has placed an unusual emphasis upon suffering.

Painful Comedy By this time the reader may feel that if *Twelfth Night* has been correctly described, if violence and grief and pain are really so important, we ought to call the play not a comedy but a tragedy. I must stress again that in picking out the non-comic features for special attention I do not wish to suggest that they are *more* important than the play's fun and laughter, only that their cumulative effect may be missed – because laughter can so easily get the better of a play's finer feelings and crowd them out. Comedy, of course, may include a vast range of moods from the lightest to the darkest, and this is why, from Shakespeare's age to our own, more and more comic 'kinds' have been invented: black comedy, dark comedy, critical comedy, tragi-comedy, free comedy, happy comedy – these are just some of the possibilities. Within a year or so of writing *Twelfth Night* Shakespeare himself remarked upon the growing fashion for new 'kinds', through Polonius, who tells Hamlet that 'the actors are come hither' with 'tragedy, comedy, history, pastoral, pastoral-comical . . . tragical-comical-historical-pastoral' and other strange hybrids. Here Shakespeare smiles at the fashion, and in doing so gives us a vital clue for the understanding of *Twelfth Night*. For there are strong reasons for believing that he wrote *Twelfth Night* after his gayest and happiest love-comedies (e.g. *A Midsummer Night's Dream*, *The Merchant of Venice*, *As You Like It*) but before most of his so-called 'dark comedies' (e.g. *All's Well that Ends Well*, *Measure for Measure*) and his tragedies. Is it not likely then that as he advanced from highly artificial 'happy comedies' to the realism and unpleasantness of the darker ones, with their emphasis on pain and treachery and sex and squalor, *Twelfth Night*, falling between the two in time, might also mediate between the two in general character? Hybrids were all the vogue, and *Twelfth Night*, neither happy nor dark but a strange, elusive mixture, goes some way towards being a hybrid – of which we are usefully reminded by adopting a 'mixed' label such as 'painful comedy'.

Nothing in *Twelfth Night*, not even its poetry, is more dazzling than the craftsmanship with which Shakespeare has so carefully concealed the joints between pain and laughter. Critics have been tempted into making rash distinctions between the main plot and underplot, calling the one sentimental and the other realistic or the like. While I would not care to argue that there are *no* differences between the two plots it is worth saying that the very lines of demarcation between them are elusive. Though I described Feste, Toby and Maria as the moving spirits of the underplot (p. 14), Shakespeare may well have thought of his story as revolving round two houses, Orsino's and Olivia's, with Viola/Orsino and Olivia/Malvolio as his two central relationships, or plots. (Notice that, until very near the end, one partner in each pair remains ignorant of the other's passion; that Viola and Olivia put up with the most extraordinary humiliations in their pursuit of love; that Orsino, like Malvolio, might be accused of being 'sick of self-love'; that Malvolio, like Orsino, suffers from an over-indulged 'fancy'; that Malvolio and Orsino both complain bitterly of ill-usage in Act V: similar repetitions or parallels, which help to unify a play, occur throughout Shakespeare.) Whether we define the underplot as centering on Olivia's house or on the lower orders within it, however, we have to admit that it binds together perfectly with what surrounds it, not only because Sir Andrew aspires (like Orsino and Malvolio) to marry Olivia, not only because Feste and Viola come and go from without, but because there are no manifest breaks in the play's make-believe. If we want to call the underplot 'realistic', citing the merry-making of Act II, scene 3 as not so very far removed from recorded anecdotes of bibbing and babbling in Elizabethan England, there is just as much realism in a noble youth's devotion to sentimental music – and indeed in Viola's dressing up as a boy. (One of Queen Elizabeth's maids of honour, it was said, used to meet her lover disguised as a page.) If the confusion of Viola and her twin brother seems wildly improbable, how much less so is a cross-gartered Malvolio, given his character? The plausibility of the action fluctuates in both plots, but the dramatist knows exactly what he can get away with, underpinning the grossest improbabilities with realistic detail (for example, the admiring incredulity of Fabian's 'If this were played upon a stage now, I could condemn it as an improbable fiction').

Main plot and underplot interpenetrate one another in theme, in the coming and going of the characters, in general plausibility – and also in their modulation of moods. 'Painful comedy' defines the whole play, not just one part of it, for many of the finer moments of this masterpiece move us like the mingling of May and December. Shakespeare clearly pondered such a 'divided response' in describing Patience on a monument *smiling at grief* (II. 4. 115), an image he seized upon also to portray Cordelia –

> patience and sorrow strove
> Who should express her goodliest. You have seen
> Sunshine and rain at once: her smiles and tears
> Were like, a better way.   (*King Lear*, IV. 3. 16–19)

In *Twelfth Night* the mixture of sunshine and rain changes perpetually. As the story moves forward the sunshine gradually fades, as may be illustrated from Malvolio's fate, or that of any of the principals. The imagery of the scene in which Malvolio finds the letter warns us that delight here borders on sadism – 'If I lose a scruple of this sport, let me be boiled to death', 'we will fool him black and blue', 'look, how imagination blows him up', 'O for a stone-bow, to hit him in the eye', 'and does not Toby take you a blow on the lips then?' Audiences laugh when Malvolio enters cross-gartered in his next scene, but we should realise, as he grins and leers at Olivia, that he does violence to his own nature, and it should give us the creeps. The dark room takes him one step lower, we laugh or smile even more uncomfortably, though Feste's fooling still lends the scene some cold, very cold, sunshine; whilst Malvolio's final appearance holds no sunshine, only rain. Viola, Olivia, Toby, and Feste all move in the same way from predominant sunshine towards the rain.

Viewing *Twelfth Night* as 'painful comedy' we find that, despite superficial resemblances, it differs profoundly from its predecessors, such as *The Merchant of Venice* and *As You Like It*. Shakespeare examines the loneliness, not the togetherness, of love. The three ladies, Viola, Olivia, and Maria, all have to pursue an unwilling mate. The men also indulge one-sided passions, notably Orsino, but also Malvolio, Sir Andrew, and, perhaps, Feste and Antonio.[1] In a

[1] For Antonio see II. 1. 34, note.

way, then, the lovers appear as predators, snatching at what they can get, because the romantic sense of mutuality has been so carefully excluded. Illyria, far from being a romantic never-never land, becomes something of a jungle, though the more cruel realities (begging for tips, scorned love, public disgrace) are covered over with songs and laughter, cakes and ale. In the sunshine of the play's earlier scenes we *may* feel that Illyria is Elysium; long before the end, however, we recognise that the psychological and intellectual uncertainties with which Shakespeare has enriched romance have brought us close to the world of Elizabethan England – the world of the 'wind and the rain'.

Date On 2 February 1602 John Manningham attended a performance of *Twelfth Night* at the Middle Temple, and scribbled some notes about it in his diary. The play will not have been more than a year or two old, at most, for it alludes to events and publications of 1599 and 1600, such as the munificence of the Shah of Persia to two English brothers (compare II. 5. 181, note), Mollineux's new map of the world (III. 2. 79), and the latest song-books (II. 3. 39, 105–15). Though none of these allusions can be regarded as certain, the cumulative evidence points to a date somewhere between 1600 and February, 1602.

The curious coincidence that Virginio Orsino, Duke of Bracciano, visited Queen Elizabeth's court in the winter of 1600–1601 has led to some speculation. The gallant duke, father of twins (a boy and a girl), received special honours from the Queen, not the least being that he stood beside her seat on Twelfth Night, 1601, during the performance of a comedy by Shakespeare's company, while she 'conversed continually' with him (presumably commenting upon the play). Could *Twelfth Night* have been composed for this splendid occasion? Leslie Hotson[1] has pleaded eloquently for the hypothesis, despite all the ob-

[1] *The First Night of Twelfth Night*, 1954.

jections to it. The news of Virginio Orsino's impending visit only reached London on Christmas Day, 1600, and Hotson therefore has to suppose that *Twelfth Night* was written and rehearsed in about ten days. Were Hotson to argue that Shakespeare merely changed the hero's name to Orsino, in a play that he had just completed, he would still fail to convince, for the notion that Olivia represents the elderly Queen ('in her youth') is too far-fetched, and even the play's Orsino cannot be thought a flattering likeness.

Neither 6 January 1601 nor 2 February 1602 seems a plausible 'first night' for *Twelfth Night*. The best explanation of the play's 'Orsino' would be that he received his name *after* Virginio Orsino's visit. The play's legal jargon might suggest that it was commissioned for the Middle Temple – until one recalls how many other plays of the period are crammed with the same phrases. If, as is possible, the play's title refers to the first night, this would have to be 6 January 1602.

Sources As already mentioned (p. 5), Shakespeare took the central story of *Twelfth Night*, involving Viola, Orsino, Olivia, and Sebastian, from Barnaby Rich's *novella* ('Apolonius and Silla', published in Rich's *Farewell to Military Profession*, 1581). He followed Rich's general plan, but changed the names and many details. For example, the source's Olivia mistakes Sebastian for Cesario, entertains Sebastian at her house, becomes pregnant, and, since he quietly disappears next day, later claims Cesario as the father of her child. Orsino, 'in a great fury', threatens to kill his page, who saves himself by convincing Olivia that he cannot be the father (by 'loosing his garments down to his stomach'). Overcome by Viola's devotion, Orsino marries her, while Sebastian turns up later and marries Olivia. In these episodes Shakespeare eliminated the sex and heightened the romance: and the romance also benefited when he changed Rich's prose into haunting poetry and gave Viola her 'poetic' personality.

Rich's story was a popular one in the sixteenth century. There were plays with the same plot in Italian, French, Spanish, and Latin, and prose narratives by Bandello (Italian, 1554) and Belleforest (French, 1579). The very first version seems to have been the Italian play *Gl'Ingannati* (1537). It is widely accepted that Shakespeare knew this play and several of its derivatives, and that his greatest debt was to Rich.

For Toby, Andrew, Maria, Feste, Fabian, and Malvolio, the underplot interlaced by Shakespeare with the romance, no very close sources have been discovered. An anecdote about the Comptroller of the Royal Household, Sir William Knollys, might have given a hint for Malvolio. (The Comptroller frowned upon noisy revellers at court, and on one occasion, when the Maids of Honour were 'frisking' in their room late at night, he tried to shame and frighten them into silence.) The characters, however, have their relatives in Shakespeare's earlier plays: Toby and Falstaff (*Henry IV*), Andrew and Slender (*The Merry Wives of Windsor*), Maria and Nerissa (*The Merchant of Venice*), Feste and Touchstone (*As You Like It*). In addition, Shakespeare went back over old ground in the devoted friend Antonio (*The Merchant of Venice*), in the disguised girl who follows her lover as a page (*The Two Gentlemen of Verona*), and in the mistaken identity of twins (*The Comedy of Errors*).

Text The only authoritative text of *Twelfth Night* was printed in Shakespeare's First Folio, a collection of thirty-six plays published in 1623, seven years after the author's death. Compared with other plays in the volume, *Twelfth Night* presents a clean text, with few serious corruptions. There are some forty or so obvious misprints, for which the usual emendations have been made in this edition (e.g. I. 2. 14 'Arion' for '*Orion*'; II. 5. 116 'staniel' for 'stallion'), and a very few more elusive cruxes (e.g. I. 3. 99–100 'curl by nature', Folio 'coole my nature'; I. 3. 135

'dun-coloured', Folio 'dam'd colour'd'; III. 2. 66 'nine', Folio 'mine').

It has been suggested that the Folio's clean text was based upon the actors' prompt-book. If so, an editor presumably went through the text, inserting the act-division, and other minor changes. Someone also softened the oaths in the play, in deference to a statute of 1606 against profanity in the theatre, substituting 'Jove' for 'God', and similar innocuous alternatives – it is to be feared that Sir Toby's verbal explosions, in particular, were sadly muffled.

Of greater literary interest than the textual changes introduced *circa* 1623 and 1606 are those indicating a possible remodelling of the plot, and of several characters. Originally Feste was intended to witness Malvolio's finding of the letter (see II. 3. 180), but Fabian took his place; Viola planned to entertain Orsino with songs and music (I. 2. 55–7), yet never does so, and, when Orsino calls for a favourite song from 'Cesario' (II. 4. 2), Curio explains that Feste, who 'should sing it', is once again 'about the house', though he serves Olivia and not Orsino. A popular explanation is that Shakespeare created Viola for a boy-actor who could sing, and that at the time of a later revival, no singing boy being available, Viola's songs were transferred to Feste. If Feste's duties were increased in this way it could also be argued that they had to be lightened elsewhere, and that Fabian was therefore brought into the box-tree scene. Or, as others have held, perhaps Feste dropped out of the box-tree scene because its boisterous humour afforded few opportunities for his subtler wit[1]. Others, again, deny the remodelling of *Twelfth Night* for a revival. Shakespeare, they say, simply changed his mind as the play grew in his hands. Whichever view we prefer, the practical effect remains the same – that some details concerning Viola, Feste and Fabian fail to fit in with the rest of the text.

[1] See also p. 11.

24

THE CHARACTERS

ORSINO, Duke of Illyria
VALENTINE ⎫
CURIO ⎭ gentlemen attending on Orsino
FIRST OFFICER
SECOND OFFICER

VIOLA ('Cesario'), a shipwrecked lady
SEBASTIAN, her twin brother
CAPTAIN of the wrecked ship
ANTONIO, another sea-captain

OLIVIA, a countess
MARIA, her waiting-gentlewoman
SIR TOBY BELCH, her uncle
SIR ANDREW AGUECHEEK, Sir Toby's friend
MALVOLIO, Olivia's steward
FABIAN, a member of Olivia's household
FESTE, Olivia's fool

A PRIEST
A SERVANT

Lords, musicians, sailors, attendants

'*Twelfth Night*' suggests either that the play was first performed on Twelfth Night (6 January), or that it represents the spirit of Twelfth Night, of revelry, when you are allowed to do '*what you will*'. But the sub-title could also mean '[Call the play] whatever you will.'

ACT ONE, scene 1

For the act-division see p. 24. Shakespeare probably only divided the play into scenes.

	Orsino *See p. 21.*
	Illyria *On the eastern side of the Adriatic (now Yugoslavia). In Shakespeare's time Illyria was ruled by Venice – hence (perhaps) the play's Italian names.*
3	appetite *love's appetite for music*
4	fall *cadence*
5	sound *music. Some editors change to* south *or* sough.
9	quick and fresh *keen and hungry*
10	capacity *power of receiving or containing*
12	validity . . . pitch *value and excellence*
13	falls . . . abatement *loses its value*
	price *esteem*
14	shapes *forms; conceptions*
	fancy *love*
15	high fantastical *highly imaginative (or capricious)*
18	the noblest *the noblest hart (heart). The heart was thought the noblest organ of the body.*
20	pestilence *plague. London was more or less clear of the plague in 1601–2, but had suffered fearfully not long before.*
22	fell *fierce*
	hounds *Alluding to Actaeon, a famous hunter who saw the goddess Diana when she was naked, was turned into a stag, and torn to pieces by his own hounds.*
24	So please *Apologetic: 'if I may be excused for saying so'.*
	might *could*
25	handmaid *Maria(?)*
26	element *sky*
	heat *Perhaps 'until seven years' heat restore her to life (from cloistering grief)'. Some emend* heat *to* hence.
28	cloistress *nun*

26

ACT ONE

Scene 1. *Music. Enter* ORSINO, *Duke of Illyria*, CURIO, *and other lords*

ORSINO   If music be the food of love, play on,
          Give me excess of it, that, surfeiting,
          The appetite may sicken, and so die.
          That strain again! It had a dying fall.
          O, it came o'er my ear like the sweet sound
          That breathes upon a bank of violets,
          Stealing and giving odour. Enough, no more!
          'Tis not so sweet now as it was before.
          O spirit of love, how quick and fresh art thou,
          That, notwithstanding thy capacity   10
          Receiveth as the sea, naught enters there,
          Of what validity and pitch soe'er,
          But falls into abatement and low price
          Even in a minute. So full of shapes is fancy
          That it alone is high fantastical.
CURIO   Will you go hunt, my lord?
ORSINO   What, Curio?
CURIO   The hart.
ORSINO   Why, so I do, the noblest that I have.
          O, when mine eyes did see Olivia first
          Methought she purged the air of pestilence.   20
          That instant was I turned into a hart,
          And my desires, like fell and cruel hounds,
          E'er since pursue me.
                 Enter VALENTINE
          How now! What news from her?
VALENTINE   So please my lord, I might not be admitted,
          But from her handmaid do return this answer:
          The element itself, till seven years' heat,
          Shall not behold her face at ample view,
          But like a cloistress she will veilèd walk,
          And water once a day her chamber round

ACT ONE, scene 2

With eye-offending brine; all this to season   30
A brother's dead love, which she would keep
    fresh
And lasting, in her sad remembrance.

ORSINO   O, she that hath a heart of that fine frame
To pay this debt of love but to a brother,
How will she love, when the rich golden shaft
Hath killed the flock of all affections else
That live in her; when liver, brain, and heart,
These sovereign thrones, are all supplied and
    filled,
Her sweet perfections, with one self king!
Away before me to sweet beds of flowers!   40
Love thoughts lie rich when canopied with
    bowers.

                                                [*Exeunt*

Scene 2. *Enter* VIOLA, *a* CAPTAIN, *and* SAILORS

VIOLA   What country, friends, is this?
CAPTAIN   This is Illyria, lady.
VIOLA   And what should I do in Illyria?
My brother, he is in Elysium.
Perchance he is not drowned. What think you,
    sailors?
CAPTAIN   It is perchance that you yourself were
    saved.
VIOLA   O, my poor brother! and so perchance may
he be.
CAPTAIN   True, madam, and to comfort you with
    chance,
Assure yourself, after our ship did split,
When you and those poor number saved with
    you
Hung on our driving boat, I saw your brother,   10
Most provident in peril, bind himself –
Courage and hope both teaching him the
    practice –

30

To a strong mast, that lived upon the sea;
Where, like Arion on the dolphin's back,
I saw him hold acquaintance with the waves
So long as I could see.
VIOLA   For saying so, there's gold.
Mine own escape unfoldeth to my hope,
Whereto thy speech serves for authority,
The like of him. Know'st thou this country?
CAPTAIN   Ay, madam, well, for I was bred and born   20
Not three hours' travel from this very place.
VIOLA   Who governs here?
CAPTAIN   A noble Duke, in nature as in name.
VIOLA   What is his name?
CAPTAIN   Orsino.
VIOLA   Orsino! I have heard my father name him:
He was a bachelor then.
CAPTAIN   And so is now, or was so, very late;
For but a month ago I went from hence,
And then 'twas fresh in murmur – as you know,   30
What great ones do, the less will prattle of –
That he did seek the love of fair Olivia.
VIOLA   What's she?
CAPTAIN   A virtuous maid, the daughter of a count
That died some twelvemonth since, then leaving
    her
In the protection of his son, her brother,
Who shortly also died; for whose dear love,
They say, she hath abjured the sight
And company of men.
VIOLA   O, that I served that lady,
And might not be delivered to the world   40
Till I had made mine own occasion mellow
What my estate is.
CAPTAIN   That were hard to compass,
Because she will admit no kind of suit,
No, not the Duke's.
VIOLA   There is a fair behaviour in thee, Captain,

31

ACT ONE, scene 3

And though that nature with a beauteous wall
Doth oft close in pollution, yet of thee
I will believe thou hast a mind that suits
With this thy fair and outward character.
I prithee – and I'll pay thee bounteously –   50
Conceal me what I am, and be my aid
For such disguise as haply shall become
The form of my intent. I'll serve this Duke.
Thou shalt present me as an eunuch to him.
It may be worth thy pains, for I can sing
And speak to him in many sorts of music.
That will allow me very worth his service.
What else may hap to time I will commit,
Only shape thou thy silence to my wit.

CAPTAIN   Be you his eunuch, and your mute I'll be.   60
When my tongue blabs, then let mine eyes not
   see.
VIOLA   I thank thee. Lead me on.

                        [Exeunt

Scene 3. *Enter* SIR TOBY BELCH *and* MARIA

SIR TOBY   What a plague means my niece to take the
death of her brother thus? I am sure care's an enemy
to life.

MARIA   By my troth, Sir Toby, you must come in
earlier o'nights. Your cousin, my lady, takes great
exceptions to your ill hours.

SIR TOBY   Why, let her except before excepted.

MARIA   Ay, but you must confine yourself within
the modest limits of order.

SIR TOBY   Confine! I'll confine myself no finer than   10
I am. These clothes are good enough to drink in, and
so be these boots too; an they be not, let them hang
themselves in their own straps.

MARIA   That quaffing and drinking will undo you.
I heard my lady talk of it yesterday, and of a foolish

| 20 | tall *big; brave* |
| | any's *any who is* |

22	ducats *Gold or silver coin of varying value in different European countries.*
23–4	Ay . . . ducats *i.e. he will squander his fortune in a year.*
24	very *perfect*
25–6	viol-de-gamboys *bass-viol*

27	without book *by heart*
29	natural *i.e. like a natural idiot*
31–3	gift . . . gift *natural ability . . . present*
31	gust *relish*
34–5	substractors *perversion of 'detractors'*

| 40 | coistrel *base rogue* |

42	parish top *A large top was apparently kept in villages for use in frosty weather, 'that the peasants might be kept warm by exercise, and out of mischief while they could not work'.*
	Castiliano vulgo *Unexplained. Perhaps Toby tells Maria to assume a grave (Castilian) expression. Castiliano could be a Spanish ducat (coin), so Toby possibly says 'I am thinking about [volgo] money!'*
47	shrew *Alluding to Maria's mouse-like size. A shrew was also a scold.*
49	Accost *A nautical term (= to greet politely).*
51	chambermaid *A lady's maid (or a female servant). She is also called a 'gentlewoman' (I. 5. 163–4).*

knight that you brought in one night here, to be her
wooer.

SIR TOBY   Who? Sir Andrew Aguecheek?

MARIA   Ay, he.

SIR TOBY   He's as tall a man as any's in Illyria.   20

MARIA   What's that to th' purpose?

SIR TOBY   Why, he has three thousand ducats a year.

MARIA   Ay, but he'll have but a year in all these
ducats. He's a very fool and a prodigal.

SIR TOBY   Fie, that you'll say so. He plays o'th' viol-
de-gamboys, and speaks three or four languages word
for word without book, and hath all the good gifts of
nature.

MARIA   He hath indeed all, most natural; for besides that he's a fool, he's a greater quarreller; and but   30
that he hath the gift of a coward to allay the gust he
hath in quarrelling, 'tis thought among the prudent
he would quickly have the gift of a grave.

SIR TOBY   By this hand, they are scoundrels and sub-
stractors that say so of him. Who are they?

MARIA   They that add, moreover, he's drunk
nightly in your company.

SIR TOBY   With drinking healths to my niece! I'll
drink to her as long as there is a passage in my throat
and drink in Illyria. He's a coward and a coistrel that   40
will not drink to my niece till his brains turn o'th'
toe, like a parish top. What, wench! *Castiliano vulgo* –
for here comes Sir Andrew Agueface!

Enter SIR ANDREW AGUECHEEK

SIR ANDREW Sir Toby Belch! How now, Sir Toby
Belch?

SIR TOBY   Sweet Sir Andrew!

SIR ANDREW Bless you, fair shrew.

MARIA   And you too, sir.

SIR TOBY   Accost, Sir Andrew, accost.

SIR ANDREW What's that?   50

SIR TOBY   My niece's chambermaid.

56, 58, 62 [Aside] *Asides are not marked in the Folio: in this passage they may not be necessary.*

57 front *confront, face (up to) her*

58 troth *faith*
undertake *engage with*

62, 64 An *If*

66 in hand *to deal with*

68 Marry *A mild oath.*

70 thought is free *The proverbial retort to those who ask 'Dost thou think me a fool?'*

71 buttery bar *Ledge at the door of the butter-hatch (on which to rest tankards).*

74 dry *thirsty; (a sign that one is) impotent*

75–6 I . . . dry *Alluding to the proverb, 'Fools have wit enough to keep dry.'*

77 dry *stupid; mocking*

79 I . . . ends *I have them always ready; I am holding them (dry jokes, i.e. your hand) with my fingers now.*

80 barren *i.e. sexually barren, after full (l. 78). She implies that she needs Sir Andrew to fertilise her wit!*

81 canary *A sweet wine from the Canary Islands.*

85 ordinary *A pun? An* ordinary *was a meal regularly available at a fixed price at an inn.*

86–7 beef . . . wit *A medical opinion at this time. 'Beef-witted' meant 'stupid'.*

36

SIR ANDREW Good Mistress Accost, I desire better acquaintance.

MARIA My name is Mary, sir.

SIR ANDREW Good Mistress Mary Accost –

SIR TOBY [*Aside*] You mistake, knight. 'Accost' is front her, board her, woo her, assail her.

SIR ANDREW [*Aside*] By my troth, I would not undertake her in this company. Is that the meaning of 'accost'?   60

MARIA Fare you well, gentlemen.

SIR TOBY [*Aside*] An thou let part so, Sir Andrew, would thou mightst never draw sword again.

SIR ANDREW An you part so, mistress, I would I might never draw sword again. Fair lady, do you think you have fools in hand?

MARIA Sir, I have not you by th' hand.

SIR ANDREW Marry, but you shall have, and here's my hand.

MARIA Now, sir, 'thought is free.' I pray you,   70
bring your hand to th' buttery bar and let it drink.

SIR ANDREW Wherefore, sweetheart? What's your metaphor?

MARIA It's dry, sir.

SIR ANDREW Why, I think so. I am not such an ass, but I can keep my hand dry. But what's your jest?

MARIA A dry jest, sir.

SIR ANDREW Are you full of them?

MARIA Ay, sir. I have them at my fingers' ends.
Marry, now I let go your hand, I am barren.   80

[*Exit*

SIR TOBY O knight, thou lack'st a cup of canary. When did I see thee so put down?

SIR ANDREW Never in your life, I think, unless you see canary put me down. Methinks sometimes I have no more wit than a Christian or an ordinary man has; but I am a great eater of beef, and I believe that does harm to my wit.

89   An *If*

91   Pourquoi *why (French)*

96–7   Then . . . hair *Toby puns on* tongues *(languages) and*
        tongs *(curling-irons).*

103   distaff *A cleft stick on which wool or flax was wound.*

104   huswife *housewife; hussy. It was believed that venereal
        disease and sexual excess caused baldness.*

108   Count *i.e. Duke*

111   estate *fortune*

112   there's . . . in't *it's not a hopeless cause*

114–15 masques . . . revels *masquerades and revelry*

116   kickshawses *trifles (French* quelque chose*)*

118   under . . . betters *i.e. as long as he is not my social
        superior*

119   old man *Is this said in deference to Toby?*

120   galliard *A lively five-step dance in which the fifth step
        was a frisky leap, or* caper.

122   mutton *Toby implies that the only capers Andrew can
        cut are those served with mutton.*

123   back-trick *Perhaps a 'reverse step in dancing', with an
        allusion to sexual prowess (taking* mutton = *prosti-
        tute).*

38

SIR TOBY   No question.

SIR ANDREW An I thought that, I'd forswear it. I'll ride
home tomorrow, Sir Toby.   90

SIR TOBY   *Pourquoi*, my dear knight?

SIR ANDREW What is *pourquoi*? Do, or not do? I would
I had bestowed that time in the tongues that I have
in fencing, dancing, and bear-baiting. O, had I but
followed the arts!

SIR TOBY   Then hadst thou had an excellent head of
hair.

SIR ANDREW Why, would that have mended my hair?

SIR TOBY   Past question, for thou seest it will not curl
by nature.   100

SIR ANDREW But it becomes me well enough, does't
not?

SIR TOBY   Excellent, it hangs like flax on a distaff;
and I hope to see a huswife take thee between her
legs and spin it off.

SIR ANDREW Faith, I'll home tomorrow, Sir Toby.
Your niece will not be seen, or if she be, it's four to
one she'll none of me; the Count himself, here hard
by, woos her.

SIR TOBY   She'll none o'th' Count; she'll not match 110
above her degree, neither in estate, years, nor wit.
I have heard her swear't. Tut, there's life in't, man.

SIR ANDREW I'll stay a month longer. I am a fellow o'th'
strangest mind i'th' world. I delight in masques and
revels sometimes altogether.

SIR TOBY   Art thou good at these kickshawses, knight?

SIR ANDREW As any man in Illyria, whatsoever he be,
under the degree of my betters, and yet I will not
compare with an old man.

SIR TOBY   What is thy excellence in a galliard, knight? 120

SIR ANDREW Faith, I can cut a caper.

SIR TOBY   And I can cut the mutton to't.

SIR ANDREW And I think I have the back-trick simply
as strong as any man in Illyria.

126   curtain *Fine pictures were sometimes protected by cur-*
              tains.

127   take *gather*
             Mistress Mall's picture *Perhaps an allusion to Mary*
             (*Mall*) *Fitton, who was involved in a court scandal in*
             1601. Or should we read Mall's mistress' picture
             (= *Maria's mistress' face*)? *Olivia says 'we will draw*
             the curtain *and show you the* picture' (*I. 5. 236–7*).

129   coranto *A fast, skipping dance.*
             jig *A lively, rapid dance.*

130   sink-apace *A five-step dance like a galliard* (*with a*
             quibble on sink = *sewer*).

131   virtues *talents*

133   star . . . galliard *a dancing star*

135   dun-coloured stock *brown-coloured stocking. For* dun
             the Folio reads dam'd: *editors emend to* dun, *damask,*
             flame, etc.

138   Taurus *The Bull, one of the twelve signs of the Zodiac,*
             each of which was supposed to influence a part of the
             human body. Different astrologers related the signs
             to different parts of the body.

ACT ONE, scene 4

5   humour *disposition*

6   that *in that*

7   love *kindness, favour*

9   Count *Duke*

11   On . . . attendance *i.e. I attend on you*

13   no . . . all *i.e. everything*

14   book *i.e. the complete statement* (*hitherto kept secret*).
             Valuable books *often had clasps at this time.*

40

SIR TOBY   Wherefore are these things hid? Wherefore have these gifts a curtain before 'em? Are they
like to take dust, like Mistress Mall's picture? Why
dost thou not go to church in a galliard and come
home in a coranto? My very walk should be a jig. I
would not so much as make water but in a sink-apace. 130
What dost thou mean? Is it a world to hide virtues
in? I did think by the excellent constitution of thy
leg it was formed under the star of a galliard.

SIR ANDREW Ay, 'tis strong, and it does indifferent well
in a dun-coloured stock. Shall we set about some
revels?

SIR TOBY   What shall we do else? Were we not born
under Taurus?

SIR ANDREW Taurus? That's sides and heart.

SIR TOBY   No, sir, it is legs and thighs. Let me see 140
thee caper. Ha! Higher! Ha! Ha! Excellent!

[*Exeunt*

Scene 4. *Enter* VALENTINE, *and* VIOLA *dressed as a man*

VALENTINE   If the Duke continue these favours towards
you, Cesario, you are like to be much advanced. He
hath known you but three days, and already you are
no stranger.

VIOLA   You either fear his humour or my negligence, that you call in question the continuance of
his love. Is he inconstant, sir, in his favours?

VALENTINE   No, believe me.

Enter ORSINO, CURIO, *and* ATTENDANTS

VIOLA   I thank you. Here comes the Count.

ORSINO   Who saw Cesario, ho?   10

VIOLA   On your attendance, my lord, here.

ORSINO   [*To* CURIO *and* ATTENDANTS] Stand you
awhile aloof. [*To* VIOLA] Cesario,
     Thou know'st no less but all. I have unclasped
     To thee the book even of my secret soul.

ACT ONE, scene 5

Therefore, good youth, address thy gait unto her.
Be not denied access; stand at her doors,
And tell them, there thy fixèd foot shall grow
Till thou have audience.

VIOLA   Sure, my noble lord,
If she be so abandoned to her sorrow   20
As it is spoke, she never will admit me.

ORSINO   Be clamorous and leap all civil bounds
Rather than make unprofited return.

VIOLA   Say I do speak with her, my lord, what
then?

ORSINO   O, then unfold the passion of my love.
Surprise her with discourse of my dear faith.
It shall become thee well to act my woes;
She will attend it better in thy youth
Than in a nuncio's of more grave aspect.   30

VIOLA   I think not so, my lord.

ORSINO   Dear lad, believe it.
For they shall yet belie thy happy years
That say thou art a man. Diana's lip
Is not more smooth and rubious. Thy small pipe
Is as the maiden's organ, shrill and sound,
And all is semblative a woman's part.
I know thy constellation is right apt
For this affair. Some four or five attend him –
All, if you will; for I myself am best
When least in company. Prosper well in this,   40
And thou shalt live as freely as thy lord,
To call his fortunes thine.

VIOLA   I'll do my best
To woo your lady. [*Aside*] Yet, a barful strife!
Whoe'er I woo, myself would be his wife.
                                        [*Exeunt*

Scene 5. *Enter* MARIA *and* FESTE

MARIA   Nay, either tell me where thou hast been,
or I will not open my lips so wide as a bristle may

43

3	in . . . excuse *to excuse you* (*to Olivia*)
	hang thee *Playful exaggeration – 'she'll murder you'.*
6	fear . . . colours *An old saying for 'fear nothing'. Feste puns on* colours *and* collars: *Maria returns to the original sense of* colours *in this saying* ('*military standards*').
7	Make . . . good *Explain* (*or prove*) *that.*
9	lenten *meagre, short*
14–15	Well . . . talents *Feste echoes 'To him that hath shall be given', and the parable of the talents.*
15	talents *Perhaps with a pun on* talent = talon (*claw*).
17	to *A '*to*' was often inserted before the second of two verbs governed by the same auxiliary.*
	turned away *dismissed*
19	Many . . . marriage *See p. 12.*
20	let . . . out *i.e. let summer weather make it endurable*
21	resolute *i.e. determined not to answer*
22	resolved *satisfied. Maria takes the word as = Latin* resolvo (*untie, loosen*).
23	points *Maria interprets as '*laces*'* (*to hold up* gaskins, *loose breeches*).
27–8	thou . . . flesh ('*you would be as witty a wife . . .*') *Hinting at Maria's later marriage* (*V. 1. 366*).
30–1	you . . . best *it would be best for you*
32	Wit *Mental powers, mind, intelligence*
	an't *if it*
35	Quinapalus *Invented by Feste to ridicule those who quote obscure authorities.*

enter, in way of thy excuse. My lady will hang thee for thy absence.

FESTE   Let her hang me. He that is well hanged in this world needs to fear no colours.

MARIA   Make that good.

FESTE   He shall see none to fear.

MARIA   A good lenten answer! I can tell thee where that saying was born, of 'I fear no colours'.   10

FESTE   Where, good Mistress Mary?

MARIA   In the wars; and that may you be bold to say in your foolery.

FESTE   Well, God give them wisdom that have it; and those that are fools, let them use their talents.

MARIA   Yet you will be hanged for being so long absent; or to be turned away – is not that as good as a hanging to you?

FESTE   Many a good hanging prevents a bad marriage; and for turning away, let summer bear it out.   20

MARIA   You are resolute, then?

FESTE   Not so neither, but I am resolved on two points.

MARIA   That if one break, the other will hold; or if both break, your gaskins fall.

FESTE   Apt, in good faith, very apt. Well, go thy way – if Sir Toby would leave drinking, thou wert as witty a piece of Eve's flesh as any in Illyria.

MARIA   Peace, you rogue, no more o'that. Here comes my lady. Make your excuse wisely, you were   30
best.   [Exit

Enter OLIVIA *with* MALVOLIO *and* ATTENDANTS

FESTE   Wit, an't be thy will, put me into good fooling. Those wits that think they have thee do very oft prove fools; and I that am sure I lack thee may pass for a wise man. For what says Quinapalus? 'Better a witty fool than a foolish wit'. God bless thee, lady!

OLIVIA   Take the fool away.

45

FESTE   Do you not hear, fellows? Take away the
lady.   40
OLIVIA   Go to, y'are a dry fool: I'll no more of you.
Besides, you grow dishonest.
FESTE   Two faults, madonna, that drink and good
counsel will amend. For give the dry fool drink, then
is the fool not dry. Bid the dishonest man mend himself: if he mend, he is no longer dishonest; if he cannot, let the botcher mend him. Anything that's
mended is but patched: virtue that transgresses is
but patched with sin; and sin that amends is but
patched with virtue. If that this simple syllogism will   50
serve, so; if it will not, what remedy? As there is no
true cuckold but calamity, so beauty's a flower. The
lady bade take away the fool; therefore I say again –
take her away!
OLIVIA   Sir, I bade them take away you.
FESTE   Misprision in the highest degree! Lady,
cucullus non facit monachum; that's as much to say as
I wear not motley in my brain. Good madonna, give
me leave to prove you a fool.
OLIVIA   Can you do it?   60
FESTE   Dexteriously, good madonna.
OLIVIA   Make your proof.
FESTE   I must catechise you for it, madonna.
Good my mouse of virtue, answer me.
OLIVIA   Well, sir, for want of other idleness, I'll
bide your proof.
FESTE   Good madonna, why mourn'st thou?
OLIVIA   Good fool, for my brother's death.
FESTE   I think his soul is in hell, madonna.
OLIVIA   I know his soul is in heaven, fool.   70
FESTE   The more fool, madonna, to mourn for
your brother's soul, being in heaven. Take away the
fool, gentlemen.
OLIVIA   What think you of this fool, Malvolio?
Doth he not mend?

76–7   Yes . . . him *i.e. he will improve in folly till death*

81   no fox *not cunning. He implies that Malvolio is a fox.*
     pass *pledge*

85   barren *i.e. witless*
     put down with *bested or silenced by*
87   he's . . . guard *he has run out of repartee (a fencing
       metaphor)*
88   minister occasion *afford opportunity*

90   set *professional, not spontaneous*
91   zanies *stooges*

93   distempered *diseased; ill-tempered*
     generous *liberal-minded*
94   free *magnanimous*
95   bird-bolts *blunt arrows*
96   allowed *licensed*
97   rail *scoff*
     a . . . man *Malvolio? If so, does she flatter or mock him?*

99   leasing *deception, lying. (Mercury was the god of decep-
       tion).*

105   well attended *i.e. he is a person of some consequence*

110   suit *petition*
111   what you will *say or do what you will. Compare the
       play's sub-title.*

48

MALVOLIO   Yes, and shall do, till the pangs of death
shake him. Infirmity, that decays the wise, doth ever
make the better fool.

FESTE   God send you, sir, a speedy infirmity for
the better increasing your folly. Sir Toby will be   80
sworn that I am no fox, but he will not pass his word
for twopence that you are no fool.

OLIVIA   How say you to that, Malvolio?

MALVOLIO   I marvel your ladyship takes delight in
such a barren rascal. I saw him put down the other
day with an ordinary fool that has no more brain
than a stone. Look you now, he's out of his guard
already; unless you laugh and minister occasion to
him, he is gagged. I protest I take these wise men,
that crow so at these set kind of fools, no better than   90
the fools' zanies.

OLIVIA   O, you are sick of self-love, Malvolio, and
taste with a distempered appetite. To be generous,
guiltless, and of free disposition, is to take those things
for bird-bolts that you deem cannon-bullets. There
is no slander in an allowed fool, though he do nothing
but rail; nor no railing in a known discreet man,
though he do nothing but reprove.

FESTE   Now Mercury endue thee with leasing, for
thou speak'st well of fools.   100

Enter MARIA

MARIA   Madam, there is at the gate a young gentleman much desires to speak with you.

OLIVIA   From the Count Orsino, is it?

MARIA   I know not, madam. 'Tis a fair young man
and well attended.

OLIVIA   Who of my people hold him in delay?

MARIA   Sir Toby, madam, your kinsman.

OLIVIA   Fetch him off, I pray you, he speaks nothing but madman. Fie on him! Go you, Malvolio. If it
be a suit from the Count, I am sick or not at home –   110
what you will, to dismiss it.   [*Exit* MALVOLIO

112	old *stale*
115	Jove *See p. 24.*
117	pia mater *brain*
122	here *Perhaps Toby strikes his chest, to indicate that one is a gentleman in one's heart. Or should we read 'Here! a plague' (Here referring to a hiccup)?*
123	pickle-herring *He pretends that he has not been drink-ing!*
	sot *fool*
125	Cousin *See I. 3. 1, note.*
126	lethargy *Presumably Toby yawns, after a late night (compare II. 3. 1).*
127	defy *reject, despise*
130	an *if*
131	faith *i.e. to resist the devil*
134	above heat *i.e. that brings him above a normal tempera-ture*
136	crowner *coroner*
137	sit o' my coz *hold an inquest on my kinsman*

Now you see, sir, how your fooling grows old and people dislike it.

FESTE   Thou hast spoke for us, madonna, as if thy eldest son should be a fool; whose skull Jove cram with brains, for – here he comes –

Enter SIR TOBY

one of thy kin has a most weak *pia mater*.

OLIVIA   By mine honour, half drunk! What is he at the gate, cousin?

SIR TOBY   A gentleman.   120

OLIVIA   A gentleman! What gentleman?

SIR TOBY   'Tis a gentleman here – a plague o'these pickle-herring! [*To* FESTE] How now, sot!

FESTE   Good Sir Toby!

OLIVIA   Cousin, cousin, how have you come so early by this lethargy?

SIR TOBY   Lechery? I defy lechery! There's one at the gate.

OLIVIA   Ay, marry, what is he?

SIR TOBY   Let him be the devil an he will, I care not. 130 Give me faith, say I. Well, it's all one.

[*Exit* SIR TOBY *followed by* MARIA

OLIVIA   What's a drunken man like, fool?

FESTE   Like a drowned man, a fool, and a madman. One draught above heat makes him a fool, the second mads him, and a third drowns him.

OLIVIA   Go thou and seek the crowner, and let him sit o' my coz, for he's in the third degree of drink – he's drowned. Go, look after him.

FESTE   He is but mad yet, madonna, and the fool shall look to the madman.   [*Exit* 140

Enter MALVOLIO

MALVOLIO   Madam, yond young fellow swears he will speak with you. I told him you were sick; he takes on him to understand so much, and therefore comes to speak with you. I told him you were asleep; he seems to have a foreknowledge of that too, and there-

fore comes to speak with you. What is to be said to him, lady? He's fortified against any denial.

OLIVIA   Tell him, he shall not speak with me.

MALVOLIO   'Has been told so; and he says he'll stand at your door like a sheriff's post and be the supporter 150 to a bench, but he'll speak with you.

OLIVIA   What kind o'man is he?

MALVOLIO   Why, of mankind.

OLIVIA   What manner of man?

MALVOLIO   Of very ill manner; he'll speak with you, will you or no.

OLIVIA   Of what personage and years is he?

MALVOLIO   Not yet old enough for a man, nor young enough for a boy; as a squash is before 'tis a peascod, or a codling when 'tis almost an apple. 'Tis with him 160 in standing water, between boy and man. He is very well-favoured, and he speaks very shrewishly. One would think his mother's milk were scarce out of him.

OLIVIA   Let him approach. Call in my gentlewoman.

MALVOLIO   Gentlewoman, my lady calls.   [*Exit*

Enter MARIA

OLIVIA   Give me my veil. Come, throw it o'er my face.

We'll once more hear Orsino's embassy.

Enter VIOLA

VIOLA   The honourable lady of the house, which is she?

OLIVIA   Speak to me, I shall answer for her. Your 170 will?

VIOLA   Most radiant, exquisite, and unmatchable beauty – I pray you, tell me if this be the lady of the house, for I never saw her. I would be loath to cast away my speech; for besides that it is excellently well penned, I have taken great pains to con it. Good beauties, let me sustain no scorn. I am very comptible, even to the least sinister usage.

OLIVIA   Whence came you, sir?

182	modest *moderate*
184	comedian *actor; a comic actor (perhaps a 'joker')*
185	heart *Term of endearment.*
185–6	yet . . . play *yet, by reason of the most malicious fortune, I protest, I am not that which I play. (Some think Viola accuses Olivia of malice).*
188	usurp *counterfeit. Viola takes the more literal sense.*
190	bestow *confer as a gift; give in marriage*
191	reserve *preserve, keep in possession*
	from . . . commission *not part of my instructions*
194–5	forgive you *excuse you from*
201–2	If . . . brief *She compares partial and complete sanity.*
202–3	'Tis . . . dialogue *i.e. I am in no mood to take part in such aimless exchanges.*
204	Will . . . sail *Perhaps Maria offers Cesario his cloak, or points to the (probably large) hat in his hand, as if it were a sail.*
205	swabber *deckhand who cleans (because Maria tries to clear Viola out of the room)*
	hull *float, drift*
206	giant *Alluding to Maria's small size, and fierceness. Giants sometimes guarded ladies in the old romances.*
207	Tell . . . messenger *i.e. Viola fears she is being dismissed, and therefore is anxious to have something definite to report*
209	courtesy *i.e. preliminary courtesy*
210	office *business*
212	taxation . . . homage *demand for a vassal's homage (payment) to his lord*
	olive *Symbol of peace.*
213	matter *sense, substance*

VIOLA   I can say little more than I have studied, 180
and that question's out of my part. Good gentle one,
give me modest assurance if you be the lady of the
house, that I may proceed in my speech.

OLIVIA   Are you a comedian?

VIOLA   No, my profound heart; and yet, by the
very fangs of malice, I swear, I am not that I play.
Are you the lady of the house?

OLIVIA   If I do not usurp myself, I am.

VIOLA   Most certain, if you are she, you do usurp
yourself; for what is yours to bestow is not yours to 190
reserve. But this is from my commission. I will on
with my speech in your praise, and then show you the
heart of my message.

OLIVIA   Come to what is important in't. I forgive
you the praise.

VIOLA   Alas, I took great pains to study it, and 'tis
poetical.

OLIVIA   It is the more like to be feigned; I pray
you, keep it in. I heard you were saucy at my gates,
and allowed your approach rather to wonder at you 200
than to hear you. If you be not mad, be gone; if you
have reason, be brief. 'Tis not that time of moon
with me, to make one in so skipping a dialogue.

MARIA   Will you hoist sail, sir? Here lies your way.

VIOLA   No, good swabber, I am to hull here a
little longer. Some mollification for your giant, sweet
lady! Tell me your mind; I am a messenger.

OLIVIA   Sure, you have some hideous matter to
deliver, when the courtesy of it is so fearful. Speak
your office.   210

VIOLA   It alone concerns your ear. I bring no over-
ture of war, no taxation of homage. I hold the olive
in my hand; my words are as full of peace as matter.

OLIVIA   Yet you began rudely. What are you?
What would you?

VIOLA   The rudeness that hath appeared in me

have I learned from my entertainment. What I am
and what I would are as secret as maidenhead; to
your ears divinity, to any others profanation.

OLIVIA   Give us the place alone.   220

[*Exeunt* MARIA *and* ATTENDANTS

We will hear this divinity. Now, sir, what is your
text?

VIOLA   Most sweet lady –

OLIVIA   A comfortable doctrine, and much may be
said of it. Where lies your text?

VIOLA   In Orsino's bosom.

OLIVIA   In his bosom! In what chapter of his
bosom?

VIOLA   To answer by the method, in the first of
his heart.   230

OLIVIA   O, I have read it; it is heresy. Have you no
more to say?

VIOLA   Good madam, let me see your face.

OLIVIA   Have you any commission from your lord
to negotiate with my face? You are now out of your
text; but we will draw the curtain and show you the
picture. Look you, sir, such a one I was this present.
Is't not well done?

VIOLA   Excellently done – if God did all.

OLIVIA   'Tis in grain, sir, 'twill endure wind and   240
weather.

VIOLA   'Tis beauty truly blent, whose red and
white
Nature's own sweet and cunning hand laid on.
Lady, you are the cruell'st she alive,
If you will lead these graces to the gave,
And leave the world no copy.

OLIVIA   O, sir, I will not be so hard-hearted. I will
give out divers schedules of my beauty. It shall be
inventoried, and every particle and utensil labelled
to my will. As, item: two lips, indifferent red; item: 250
two grey eyes, with lids to them; item: one neck, one

57

252   praise *appraise; commend*

254   if *even if*

256–7   Could . . . beauty! *i.e. could not be overpaid even though you were acclaimed the (lady) unequalled in beauty*

258   fertile *copious*

263   In . . . divulged *i.e. well spoken of*
          free *honourable*
265   gracious *attractive*

271   willow *The emblem of disappointed love.*
272   my soul *i.e. Olivia*
273   cantons *songs*
          contemnèd *scorned*
275   Hallow *Shout*
          reverberate *reverberating*
276   gossip *tattling woman, i.e. echo*

279   But *Unless*

281   state *position in the world*

chin, and so forth. Were you sent hither to praise me?

VIOLA   I see you what you are, you are too proud.
But if you were the devil, you are fair.
My lord and master loves you – O, such love
Could be but recompensed, though you were
   crowned
The nonpareil of beauty!

OLIVIA   How does he love me?

VIOLA   With adorations, fertile tears,
With groans that thunder love, with sighs of fire.

OLIVIA   Your lord does know my mind, I cannot
   love him.   260
Yet I suppose him virtuous, know him noble,
Of great estate, of fresh and stainless youth,
In voices well divulged, free, learned, and valiant,
And in dimension and the shape of nature
A gracious person. But yet I cannot love him.
He might have took his answer long ago.

VIOLA   If I did love you in my master's flame,
With such a suff'ring, such a deadly life,
In your denial I would find no sense;
I would not understand it.

OLIVIA   Why, what would you?   270

VIOLA   Make me a willow cabin at your gate,
And call upon my soul within the house;
Write loyal cantons of contemnèd love
And sing them loud even in the dead of night;
Hallow your name to the reverberate hills
And make the babbling gossip of the air
Cry out 'Olivia!' O, you should not rest
Between the elements of air and earth,
But you should pity me.

OLIVIA   You might do much.
What is your parentage?   280

VIOLA   Above my fortunes, yet my state is well.
I am a gentleman.

OLIVIA   Get you to your lord.

287   fee'd post *messenger who accepts tips*

289   Love make *May the god of love make*
           that *whom*

296   blazon *coat of arms, i.e. gentlemanly status*

303   peevish *obstinate, ill-bred*
304   County's *Count's*
305   Would I *Whether I would*
306   flatter with *encourage*

309   Hie *Haste*

312   Mine . . . mind *i.e. my eye will overbear my judgement*
313   owe *own*

I cannot love him. Let him send no more –
Unless, perchance, you come to me again
To tell me how he takes it. Fare you well.
I thank you for your pains. Spend this for me.

VIOLA   I am no fee'd post, lady; keep your purse.
My master, not myself, lacks recompense.
Love make his heart of flint, that you shall love,
And let your fervour like my master's be   290
Placed in contempt. Farewell, fair cruelty! [*Exit*

OLIVIA   'What is your parentage?'
'Above my fortunes, yet my state is well.
I am a gentleman.' I'll be sworn thou art!
Thy tongue, thy face, thy limbs, actions, and
     spirit
Do give thee fivefold blazon. Not too fast! soft,
     soft –
Unless the master were the man. How now?
Even so quickly may one catch the plague?
Methinks I feel this youth's perfections
With an invisible and subtle stealth   300
To creep in at mine eyes. Well, let it be!
What ho, Malvolio!

                    Enter MALVOLIO

MALVOLIO   Here, madam, at your service.
OLIVIA   Run after that same peevish messenger,
The County's man. He left this ring behind him,
Would I or not. Tell him I'll none of it.
Desire him not to flatter with his lord,
Nor hold him up with hopes; I am not for him.
If that the youth will come this way tomorrow
I'll give him reasons for't. Hie thee, Malvolio!
MALVOLIO   Madam, I will.   [*Exit* 310
OLIVIA   I do I know not what, and fear to find
Mine eye too great a flatterer for my mind.
Fate, show thy force; ourselves we do not owe.
What is decreed must be, and be this so.

                                        [*Exit*

ACT TWO, scene 1

ACT TWO

Scene 1. *Enter* ANTONIO *and* SEBASTIAN

ANTONIO   Will you stay no longer? Nor will you not
that I go with you?

SEBASTIAN   By your patience, no. My stars shine darkly
over me. The malignancy of my fate might perhaps
distemper yours; therefore I shall crave of you your
leave, that I may bear my evils alone. It were a bad
recompense for your love to lay any of them on you.

ANTONIO   Let me yet know of you whither you are
bound.

SEBASTIAN   No, sooth, sir; my determinate voyage is   10
mere extravagancy. But I perceive in you so excellent
a touch of modesty, that you will not extort from me
what I am willing to keep in; therefore it charges me
in manners the rather to express myself. You must
know of me then, Antonio, my name is Sebastian,
which I called Roderigo. My father was that Sebastian of Messaline whom I know you have heard of.
He left behind him myself and a sister, both born in
an hour. If the heavens had been pleased, would we
had so ended! But you, sir, altered that, for some   20
hour before you took me from the breach of the sea
was my sister drowned.

ANTONIO   Alas the day!

SEBASTIAN   A lady, sir, though it was said she much
resembled me, was yet of many accounted beautiful.
But though I could not with such estimable wonder
over-far believe that, yet thus far I will boldly pub-
lish her: she bore a mind that envy could not but call
fair. She is drowned already, sir, with salt water,
though I seem to drown her remembrance again with   30
more.

ANTONIO   Pardon me, sir, your bad entertainment.

SEBASTIAN   O good Antonio, forgive me your trouble.

34	murder me *i.e. by parting from me. Antonio and Sebastian both speak with the extravagant courtesy of the time. Later Antonio's extravagance becomes more marked, and perhaps parallels Orsino's infatuation for 'Cesario': see l. 46, III. 3. 4, V. 1. 76.*
37	recovered *saved*
	desire *request*
38–9	kindness *affection*
40–1	tell . . . me *give me away*

ACT TWO, scene 2

1	even *just*
4	but hither *only here*
8	desperate assurance *hopeless certainty*
9	hardy *bold*
11	Receive . . . so *Take it on that understanding. Or perhaps Viola draws back her hand, Malvolio says 'Receive it!' and then '— So!' indignantly, as the ring falls to the ground.*
12	She . . . me *Viola quickly covers up Olivia's indiscretion.*
13	peevishly *perversely*
15	eye *sight*

64

ANTONIO   If you will not murder me for my love, let
   me be your servant.
SEBASTIAN   If you will not undo what you have done –
   that is, kill him whom you have recovered – desire it
   not. Fare ye well at once; my bosom is full of kind-
   ness, and I am yet so near the manners of my mother
   that, upon the least occasion more, mine eyes will tell   40
   tales of me. I am bound to the Count Orsino's court.
   Farewell.   [*Exit*
ANTONIO   The gentleness of all the gods go with
            thee!
   I have many enemies in Orsino's court,
   Else would I very shortly see thee there.
   But come what may, I do adore thee so
   That danger shall seem sport, and I will go!
                                                 [*Exit*

Scene 2. *Enter* VIOLA *and* MALVOLIO *at different doors*

MALVOLIO   Were not you even now with the Countess
   Olivia?
VIOLA   Even now, sir; on a moderate pace I have
   since arrived but hither.
MALVOLIO   She returns this ring to you, sir. You might
   have saved me my pains, to have taken it away yourself. She adds, moreover, that you should put your
   lord into a desperate assurance she will none of him.
   And one thing more, that you be never so hardy to
   come again in his affairs – unless it be to report your   10
   lord's taking of this. Receive it so.
VIOLA   She took the ring of me, I'll none of it.
MALVOLIO   Come, sir, you peevishly threw it to her,
   and her will is it should be so returned. If it be worth
   stooping for, there it lies in your eye; if not, be it his
   that finds it.   [*Exit*

19	made . . . me *looked at me closely*
20	lost *caused the loss of; destroyed*
22	cunning *craftiness*
23	Invites *Tries to attract*
25	the man *i.e. whom she loves*
28	pregnant enemy *ready, wily enemy (Satan)*
29	proper false *handsome deceivers*
31–2	Alas . . . be *Alas, our frailty is the cause, not we ourselves, for what happens to us, if we are like that.*
33	fadge *turn out*
34	monster *i.e. being neither man nor woman* fond *dote*
39	thriftless *unavailing*

ACT TWO, scene 3

2	betimes *early*
2–3	diluculo surgere *to rise at dawn (is most healthy). A well-known Latin tag.*
4	troth *faith*

VIOLA   I left no ring with her; what means this
              lady?
              Fortune forbid my outside have not charmed
              her!
              She made good view of me, indeed so much
              That, methought, her eyes had lost her tongue,   20
              For she did speak in starts, distractedly.
              She loves me, sure; the cunning of her passion
              Invites me in this churlish messenger.
              None of my lord's ring? Why, he sent her none.
              I am the man! If it be so – as 'tis –
              Poor lady, she were better love a dream.
              Disguise, I see thou art a wickedness
              Wherein the pregnant enemy does much.
              How easy is it for the proper false
              In women's waxen hearts to set their forms.   30
              Alas, our frailty is the cause, not we,
              For such as we are made, if such we be.
              How will this fadge? My master loves her dearly;
              And I, poor monster, fond as much on him;
              And she, mistaken, seems to dote on me.
              What will become of this? As I am man,
              My state is desperate for my master's love.
              As I am woman – now, alas the day –
              What thriftless sighs shall poor Olivia breathe!
              O time, thou must untangle this, not I!   40
              It is too hard a knot for me t'untie.   *[Exit*

Scene 3. *Enter* SIR TOBY *and* SIR ANDREW

SIR TOBY   Approach, Sir Andrew. Not to be abed
    after midnight, is to be up betimes, and *diluculo sur-*
    gere, thou know'st –
SIR ANDREW Nay, by my troth, I know not; but I know
    to be up late is to be up late.
SIR TOBY   A false conclusion! I hate it as an unfilled
    can. To be up after midnight and to go to bed then is

9	Does . . . lives *False concord (not unusual in Shake-speare).*
9–10	four elements *i.e. air, fire, earth, water, the simple sub-stances of which all material bodies were thought to be compounded.*
14	Marian *Maria. Compare l. 123.*
	stoup *large cup, jug*
17	We Three *i.e. a picture of two ass-heads, the spectator making the third. Feste means 'you are fools like me', Toby replies 'you have confessed to being an ass.'*
18	catch *round, part-song*
19	troth *faith*
20	breast *singing voice*
21	leg *the bow with which he begins his song(?)*
22	sooth *truth*
	gracious *pleasing*
23–4	Pigrogromitus, Vapians, Queubus *Invented names.*
25	leman *sweetheart*
26	impeticos thy gratillity *i.e. pocket or impetticoat your gratuity (tip). Fools wore long coats or 'petticoats'.*
27	whipstock *whip-handle*
28	Myrmidons *Inhabitants of Thessaly; slang for 'faithful follower'. The implications (if any) of this sentence are lost.*
33	testril *tester, sixpence*
34	a- *Either Feste interrupts, or a line is lost here.*
36	good life *moral behaviour; good company(?)*
39	O . . . mine *Shakespeare seems to have re-written a popular song (an instrumental version with the title O mistress mine was published in 1599). Some think Feste sings of Olivia, but, if he has a particular mistress in mind, it is more likely to be his leman (II. 3. 25).*
42	trip *skip, dance*
	sweeting *sweet one*

68

early; so that to go to bed after midnight is to go to
bed betimes. Does not our lives consist of the four
elements?   10

SIR ANDREW Faith, so they say; but I think it rather
consists of eating and drinking.

SIR TOBY   Thou'rt a scholar. Let us therefore eat and
drink. Marian, I say! A stoup of wine!

Enter FESTE

SIR ANDREW Here comes the fool, i'faith.

FESTE   How now, my hearts! Did you never see
. the picture of We Three?

SIR TOBY   Welcome, ass! Now let's have a catch.

SIR ANDREW By my troth, the fool has an excellent
breast. I had rather than forty shillings I had such a   20
leg, and so sweet a breath to sing, as the fool has. In
sooth, thou wast in very gracious fooling last night,
when thou spok'st of Pigrogromitus, of the Vapians
passing the equinoctial of Queubus. 'Twas very good,
i'faith. I sent thee sixpence for thy leman, hadst it?

FESTE   I did impeticos thy gratillity; for Malvolio's nose is no whipstock, my lady has a white
hand, and the Myrmidons are no bottle-ale houses.

SIR ANDREW Excellent! Why, this is the best fooling,
when all is done. Now, a song!   30

SIR TOBY   Come on, there is sixpence for you. Let's
have a song.

SIR ANDREW There's a testril of me, too. If one knight
give a –

FESTE   Would you have a love song, or a song of
good life?

SIR TOBY   A love song! A love song!

SIR ANDREW Ay, ay, I care not for good life.

FESTE [*Sings*]
        O mistress mine! Where are you roaming?
        O, stay and hear: your true love's coming,   40
            That can sing both high and low.
        Trip no further, pretty sweeting;

69

44   Every . . . know *i.e. every fool knows. Alluding to the saying that wise men have fools for their sons.*

49   still *always*

51   sweet and twenty *sweetest one;* and twenty *is an intensive, as in* Merry Wives, *II. 1. 177 'good even and twenty, Master Page'.*

54ff.   contagious breath *catchy song.* Contagious *usually meant pestilential, and Toby may here lead on Andrew to use a word he doesn't understand.*

56   by the nose *i.e. since we speak of hearing by the nose, it is sweet in its (a) catchiness (b) poison*

57   welkin *sky*

58   catch *round*

59   draw . . . weaver *Weavers were often Puritans at this time, and sang psalms, not catches. To 'draw the soul out of' = to move intensely. Some think that Toby alludes to the medieval philosophers who held that a man has three souls (vegetable, animal, rational).*

61   An *If*

           dog at *clever at*

63   dogs *Mechanical devices (with a tooth or claw) used for gripping, clamps.*

67   'Hold . . . peace' *A round with this title was published in 1609. Each singer calls the others knave in turn.*

> Journeys end in lovers meeting,
> > Every wise man's son doth know.

SIR ANDREW Excellent good, i'faith.

SIR TOBY Good, good.

FESTE [*Sings*]

> > What is love? 'Tis not hereafter;
> > Present mirth hath present laughter,
> > > What's to come is still unsure.
> > In delay there lies no plenty –
> > Then come kiss me, sweet and twenty,
> > > Youth's a stuff will not endure.

50

SIR ANDREW A mellifluous voice, as I am true knight.

SIR TOBY A contagious breath.

SIR ANDREW Very sweet and contagious, i'faith.

SIR TOBY To hear by the nose, it is dulcet in contagion. But shall we make the welkin dance indeed? Shall we rouse the night-owl in a catch that will draw three souls out of one weaver? Shall we do that?

60

SIR ANDREW An you love me, let's do't. I am dog at a catch.

FESTE By'r lady, sir, and some dogs will catch well.

SIR ANDREW Most certain. Let our catch be 'Thou knave'.

FESTE 'Hold thy peace, thou knave', knight? I shall be constrained in't to call thee knave, knight.

SIR ANDREW 'Tis not the first time I have constrained one to call me knave. Begin, fool; it begins [*he sings*] 'Hold thy peace –'

70

FESTE I shall never begin if I hold my peace.

SIR ANDREW Good, i'faith. Come begin!

> *They sing the catch*
> *Enter* MARIA

MARIA What a caterwauling do you keep here! If my lady have not called up her steward Malvolio and bid him turn you out of doors, never trust me.

SIR TOBY   My lady's a Cataian, we are politicians,
Malvolio's a Peg-a-Ramsey, and [*he sings*] 'Three
merry men be we!' Am not I consanguineous? Am I
not of her blood? Tilly-vally! 'Lady'! [*He sings*]   80
'There dwelt a man in Babylon, lady, lady –'

FESTE   Beshrew me, the knight's in admirable
fooling.

SIR ANDREW   Ay, he does well enough if he be disposed,
and so do I too. He does it with a better grace, but I
do it more natural.

SIR TOBY [*Sings*]
    'O' the twelfth day of December –'

MARIA   For the love o'God, peace!

Enter MALVOLIO

MALVOLIO   My masters, are you mad? Or what are
you? Have you no wit, manners, nor honesty, but to   90
gabble like tinkers at this time of night? Do ye make
an ale-house of my lady's house, that ye squeak out
your coziers' catches without any mitigation or re-
morse of voice? Is there no respect of place, persons,
nor time in you?

SIR TOBY   We did keep time, sir, in our catches.
Sneck up!

MALVOLIO   Sir Toby, I must be round with you. My
lady bade me tell you that, though she harbours you
as her kinsman, she's nothing allied to your disorders.   100
If you can separate yourself and your misdemeanours,
you are welcome to the house. If not, an it would
please you to take leave of her, she is very willing to
bid you farewell.

SIR TOBY [*Sings*]
    'Farewell, dear heart, since I must needs be
        gone –'

MARIA   Nay, good Sir Toby!

FESTE [*Sings*]
    'His eyes do show his days are almost done –'

MALVOLIO   Is't even so!

110   Sir . . . lie *Perhaps Toby falls down.*

113   an if *if*

116   Out . . . lie *He remembers dimly that Malvolio (l. 90 ff.)
        criticised his singing.*
118–19 cakes and ale *i.e. jollity. The Puritans objected to
        feasting at Twelfth Night etc.*
120   ginger *used to spice the ale*

123   rub . . . crumbs *i.e. keep your place (polish your ste-
        ward's chain)*

126   give . . . rule *i.e. provide drink for this outrageous carry-
        on*

128   Go . . . ears *An expression of contempt.*

130   to . . . field *i.e. to a duel. But how many knights would
        challenge a steward?*

138–9   gull . . . nayword *trick him so that he becomes a byword*
139   recreation *diversion*

74

SIR TOBY [*Sings*]
    'But I will never die –'
FESTE [*Sings*]
    'Sir Toby, there you lie –'
MALVOLIO   This is much credit to you!
SIR TOBY [*Sings*]
    'Shall I bid him go?'
FESTE [*Sings*]
    'What an if you do?'
SIR TOBY [*Sings*]
    'Shall I bid him go and spare not?'
FESTE [*Sings*]
    'O no, no, no, no, you dare not!'
SIR TOBY   [*To* MALVOLIO] Out o'tune, sir? Ye lie. Art any more than a steward? Dost thou think, because thou art virtuous, there shall be no more cakes and ale?
FESTE   Yes, by Saint Anne, and ginger shall be hot 120 i'th' mouth, too.
SIR TOBY   Th'art i'th'right. [*To* MALVOLIO] Go, sir, rub your chain with crumbs. A stoup of wine, Maria!
MALVOLIO   Mistress Mary, if you prized my lady's favour at anything more than contempt, you would not give means for this uncivil rule. She shall know of it, by this hand!   [*Exit*
MARIA   Go, shake your ears.
SIR ANDREW   'Twere as good a deed as to drink when a man's a-hungry, to challenge him the field and 130 then to break promise with him and make a fool of him.
SIR TOBY   Do't, knight, I'll write thee a challenge; or I'll deliver thy indignation to him by word of mouth.
MARIA   Sweet Sir Toby, be patient for tonight. Since the youth of the Count's was today with my lady, she is much out of quiet. For Monsieur Malvolio, let me alone with him. If I do not gull him into a nayword, and make him a common recreation, do

not think I have wit enough to lie straight in my bed. 140
I know I can do it.

SIR TOBY   Possess us, possess us, tell us something of
him.

MARIA   Marry, sir, sometimes he is a kind of
Puritan –

SIR ANDREW O, if I thought that, I'd beat him like a dog.

SIR TOBY   What, for being a Puritan? Thy exquisite
reason, dear knight?

SIR ANDREW I have no exquisite reason for't, but I have
reason good enough.   150

MARIA   The devil a Puritan that he is, or anything,
constantly, but a time-pleaser, an affectioned ass that
cons state without book and utters it by great swarths;
the best persuaded of himself, so crammed, as he
thinks, with excellencies, that it is his grounds of
faith that all that look on him love him – and on that
vice in him will my revenge find notable cause to
work.

SIR TOBY   What wilt thou do?

MARIA   I will drop in his way some obscure 160
epistles of love; wherein, by the colour of his beard,
the shape of his leg, the manner of his gait, the ex-
pressure of his eye, forehead, and complexion, he shall
find himself most feelingly personated. I can write
very like my lady, your niece; on a forgotten matter
we can hardly make distinction of our hands.

SIR TOBY   Excellent! I smell a device.

SIR ANDREW I have't in my nose too.

SIR TOBY   He shall think by the letters that thou wilt
drop that they come from my niece, and that she's in 170
love with him.

MARIA   My purpose is indeed a horse of that
colour.

SIR ANDREW And your horse now would make him an
ass.

MARIA   Ass . . . I doubt not.

ACT TWO, scene 4

SIR ANDREW O, 'twill be admirable!

MARIA   Sport royal, I warrant you. I know my
physic will work with him. I will plant you two, and
let the fool make a third, where he shall find the 180
letter. Observe his construction of it. For this night,
to bed, and dream on the event. Farewell.   [*Exit*

SIR TOBY   Good night, Penthesilea.

SIR ANDREW Before me, she's a good wench.

SIR TOBY   She's a beagle, true bred, and one that
adores me – what o'that?

SIR ANDREW I was adored once, too.

SIR TOBY   Let's to bed, knight. Thou hadst need send
for more money.

SIR ANDREW If I cannot recover your niece, I am a foul 190
way out.

SIR TOBY   Send for money, knight. If thou hast her
not i'th'end, call me cut.

SIR ANDREW If I do not, never trust me, take it how you
will.

SIR TOBY   Come, come, I'll go burn some sack, 'tis
too late to go to bed now. Come, knight; come, knight.
                                        [*Exeunt*

Scene 4. *Enter* ORSINO, VIOLA, CURIO, *and others*

ORSINO   Give me some music! Now, good morrow,
                 friends!
              Now, good Cesario, but that piece of song,
              That old and antique song we heard last night.
              Methought it did relieve my passion much,
              More than light airs and recollected terms
              Of these most brisk and giddy-pacèd times.
              Come, but one verse.

CURIO   He is not here, so please your lordship,
that should sing it.

ORSINO   Who was it?   10

79

11   fool *i e. a professional 'fool'*

18   Unstaid *Unrestrained*
          motions *emotions*
19   image *idea*

21   seat *i.e. the heart*

24   stayed *attended, waited*
          favour *face; charm*

25   by . . . favour *if you will allow me to say so (with quibble
          on favour, l. 24)*

26   complexion *nature, temperament; looks*

29   still *always*

30   An . . . herself *Could Shakespeare have forgotten his
          own marriage?*
          wears *adapts herself*
31   sways she level *swings she steady. (Her husband's love
          remains steady.)*
33   fancies *loves*
34   worn *exhausted*

37   hold . . . bent *maintain its strength (like a bent bow)*

39   displayed *unfolded; revealed*

80

CURIO   Feste the jester, my lord, a fool that the
Lady Olivia's father took much delight in. He is about
the house.

ORSINO   Seek him out, and play the tune the while.

[*Exit* CURIO

Music plays

Come hither, boy. If ever thou shalt love,
In the sweet pangs of it remember me.
For such as I am, all true lovers are:
Unstaid and skittish in all motions else
Save in the constant image of the creature
That is beloved. How dost thou like this tune?   20

VIOLA   It gives a very echo to the seat
Where love is throned.

ORSINO   Thou dost speak masterly.
My life upon't, young though thou art, thine eye
Hath stayed upon some favour that it loves.
Hath it not, boy?

VIOLA   A little, by your favour.

ORSINO   What kind of woman is't?

VIOLA   Of your complexion.

ORSINO   She is not worth thee, then. What years,
      i'faith?

VIOLA   About your years, my lord.

ORSINO   Too old, by heaven. Let still the woman
      take
An elder than herself; so wears she to him;   30
So sways she level in her husband's heart.
For, boy, however we do praise ourselves,
Our fancies are more giddy and unfirm,
More longing, wavering, sooner lost and worn,
Than women's are.

VIOLA   I think it well, my lord.

ORSINO   Then let thy love be younger than thyself,
Or thy affection cannot hold the bent.
For women are as roses whose fair flower,
Being once displayed, doth fall that very hour.

41   even *just*

44   spinsters *spinners*
45   free *unattached; carefree*
          bones *bone bobbins (for making lace)*
46   silly sooth *simple truth*

48   Like . . . age *As in the good old times.*

51   cypress *A coffin of cypress wood, or one decorated with
          cypress boughs.*
52   Fie away *Be off. Often emended to 'fly away'.*

54-5   My . . . it *No one so faithful ever partook of my allotted
          portion, death.*

60   greet *Perhaps a pun on greet = bewail.*

66   pains *trouble. Perhaps alluding to the* pains *of the lover
          in the song (that is, his anguish).*

82

VIOLA   And so they are. Alas, that they are so,   40
                 To die, even when they to perfection grow.
                        Enter CURIO *and* FESTE
ORSINO   O, fellow, come, the song we had last night.
                 Mark it, Cesario; it is old and plain.
                 The spinsters and the knitters in the sun
                 And the free maids that weave their thread with
                     bones
                 Do use to chant it. It is silly sooth,
                 And dallies with the innocence of love
                 Like the old age.
FESTE   Are you ready, sir?
ORSINO   Ay, prithee sing.

                        Music

FESTE [*Sings*]
                 Come away, come away, death,   50
                     And in sad cypress let me be laid.
                 Fie away, fie away, breath!
                     I am slain by a fair cruel maid.
                 My shroud of white, stuck all with yew,
                     O, prepare it!
                 My part of death, no one so true
                     Did share it.

                 Not a flower, not a flower sweet
                     On my black coffin let there be strewn.
                 Not a friend, not a friend greet   60
                     My poor corpse, where my bones shall be
                         thrown.
                 A thousand thousand sighs to save,
                     Lay me, O, where
                 Sad true lover never find my grave
                     To weep there.
ORSINO   [*Giving money*] There's for thy pains.
FESTE   No pains, sir. I take pleasure in singing, sir.
ORSINO   I'll pay thy pleasure, then.

                                                        83

69   pleasure . . . paid *Proverbial.*

71   leave, to leave *A polite dismissal, as if Feste were
        the master.*

72   the . . . god *Saturn, whose planet governed those of a
        melancholy humour.*

73   doublet *Close-fitting body garment.*
        changeable *Varying in colour in different lights, 'shot'.*
        taffeta *A lustrous kind of silk.*

74   opal *A semi-precious stone which changes its colour with
        the light.*

74-7   I . . . nothing *i.e. the captain of a ship willing to do
        everything and to go everywhere will have a good
        voyage though he starts with nothing.*

79   give place *withdraw*

80   sovereign cruelty *lady of supreme cruelty*

83   parts *gifts, portions (i.e. possessions)*

84   hold *value*
        giddily . . . fortune *lightly, indifferently as fortune does*

85   that miracle *i.e. her beauty*

86   pranks her in *adorns her with*

88   I *The Folio has* It, *retained by some editors.*
        Sooth *Indeed*

94   Can bide *Which can bear*

96   retention *ability to retain (medical term)*

98   No . . . liver *Not an impulse of the liver (the seat of
        passion, it was thought, and an organ that helps
        digestion)*

99   revolt *revulsion*

101   compare *comparison*

84

FESTE   Truly, sir, and pleasure will be paid, one
time or another.   70
ORSINO   Give me now leave, to leave thee.
FESTE   Now the melancholy god protect thee, and
the tailor make thy doublet of changeable taffeta, for
thy mind is a very opal. I would have men of such
constancy put to sea, that their business might be
everything, and their intent everywhere; for that's it
that always makes a good voyage of nothing. Fare-
well.   [*Exit*
ORSINO   Let all the rest give place.
                    [CURIO *and* ATTENDANTS *withdraw*
                         Once more, Cesario,
Get thee to yond same sovereign cruelty.   80
Tell her my love, more noble than the world,
Prizes not quantity of dirty lands.
The parts that fortune hath bestowed upon
     her
Tell her I hold as giddily as fortune.
But 'tis that miracle and queen of gems
That nature pranks her in, attracts my soul.
VIOLA   But if she cannot love you, sir?
ORSINO   I cannot be so answered.
VIOLA   Sooth, but you must.
Say that some lady, as perhaps there is,
Hath for your love as great a pang of heart   90
As you have for Olivia. You cannot love her.
You tell her so. Must she not then be answered?
ORSINO   There is no woman's sides
Can bide the beating of so strong a passion
As love doth give my heart; no woman's heart
So big to hold so much. They lack retention.
Alas, their love may be called appetite,
No motion of the liver, but the palate,
That suffer surfeit, cloyment, and revolt;
But mine is all as hungry as the sea,   100
And can digest as much. Make no compare

85

ACT TWO, scene 5

86

Between that love a woman can bear me
And that I owe Olivia.

VIOLA   Ay, but I know –

ORSINO   What dost thou know?

VIOLA   Too well what love women to men may
                owe.
In faith, they are as true of heart as we.
My father had a daughter loved a man –
As it might be, perhaps, were I a woman,
I should your lordship.

ORSINO   And what's her history?

VIOLA   A blank, my lord. She never told her love,   110
But let concealment, like a worm i'th'bud,
Feed on her damask cheek. She pined in thought,
And with a green and yellow melancholy
She sat like Patience on a monument
Smiling at grief. Was not this love indeed?
We men may say more, swear more, but indeed
Our shows are more than will; for still we prove
Much in our vows, but little in our love.

ORSINO   But died thy sister of her love, my boy?

VIOLA   I am all the daughters of my father's house,   120
And all the brothers too; and yet, I know not.
Sir, shall I to this lady?

ORSINO   Ay, that's the theme.
To her in haste; give her this jewel; say
My love can give no place, bide no denay.

                                        [Exeunt

Scene 5. *Enter* SIR TOBY, SIR ANDREW, *and* FABIAN

SIR TOBY   Come thy ways, Signor Fabian.

FABIAN   Nay, I'll come. If I lose a scruple of this
sport, let me be boiled to death with melancholy.

SIR TOBY   Wouldst thou not be glad to have the nig-
gardly, rascally sheep-biter come by some notable
shame?

88

FABIAN   I would exult, man. You know he brought
me out o'favour with my lady about a bear-baiting
here.

SIR TOBY   To anger him, we'll have the bear again,   10
and we will fool him black and blue – shall we not,
Sir Andrew?

SIR ANDREW An we do not, it is pity of our lives.

Enter MARIA

SIR TOBY   Here comes the little villain. How now,
my metal of India?

MARIA   Get ye all three into the box-tree. Malvolio's coming down this walk, he has been yonder
i'the sun practising behaviour to his own shadow this
half-hour. Observe him, for the love of mockery, for
I know this letter will make a contemplative idiot of   20
him. Close, in the name of jesting!

The men hide. MARIA *drops a letter*

Lie thou there – for here comes the trout that must
be caught with tickling.   [*Exit*

Enter MALVOLIO

MALVOLIO   'Tis but fortune, all is fortune. Maria once
told me she did affect me; and I have heard herself
come thus near, that should she fancy, it should be
one of my complexion. Besides, she uses me with a
more exalted respect than anyone else that follows
her. What should I think on't?

SIR TOBY   Here's an overweening rogue!   30

FABIAN   O, peace! Contemplation makes a rare
turkey-cock of him; how he jets under his advanced
plumes!

SIR ANDREW 'Slight, I could so beat the rogue!

SIR TOBY   Peace, I say!

MALVOLIO   To be Count Malvolio . . .

SIR TOBY   Ah, rogue!

SIR ANDREW Pistol him, pistol him!

SIR TOBY   Peace, peace!

MALVOLIO There is example for't. The lady of the 40
Strachy married the yeoman of the wardrobe.

SIR ANDREW Fie on him, Jezebel!

FABIAN O, peace! Now he's deeply in. Look how
imagination blows him.

MALVOLIO Having been three months married to her,
sitting in my state . . .

SIR TOBY O for a stonebow to hit him in the eye!

MALVOLIO Calling my officers about me, in my
branched velvet gown, having come from a day-bed,
where I have left Olivia sleeping . . . 50

SIR TOBY Fire and brimstone!

FABIAN O, peace, peace!

MALVOLIO And then to have the humour of state;
and after a demure travel of regard – telling them I
know my place, as I would they should do theirs – to
ask for my kinsman Toby.

SIR TOBY Bolts and shackles!

FABIAN O, peace, peace, peace! Now, now!

MALVOLIO Seven of my people with an obedient start
make out for him. I frown the while, and perchance 60
wind up my watch, or play with my [*Touching his
steward's chain*] – some rich jewel. Toby approaches,
curtsies there to me . . .

SIR TOBY Shall this fellow live?

FABIAN Though our silence be drawn from us with
cars, yet peace!

MALVOLIO I extend my hand to him thus, quenching
my familiar smile with an austere regard of control . . .

SIR TOBY And does not Toby take you a blow o'the
lips then? 70

MALVOLIO Saying, Cousin Toby, my fortunes having
cast me on your niece give me this prerogative of
speech . . .

SIR TOBY What, what!

MALVOLIO You must amend your drunkenness.

SIR TOBY Out, scab!

91

77	sinews *i.e. mainstay*
79–80	treasure . . . time *It was a Puritan commonplace that time was a treasure, and should be spent profitably.*
84	employment *business, matter*
86	woodcock *A proverbially foolish bird.* gin *snare*
87–8	the . . . him *i.e. may he take it into his head to read aloud*
90–1	C's . . . P's *These letters do not all occur in the super-scription, but are introduced to make Malvolio sound bawdy. Cut is the female organ; makes P's = urinates.*
91	in . . . question *beyond all doubts*
95	Soft *Gently* impressure *seal* Lucrece *i.e. the seal depicts Lucretia, the Roman matron famous for her chastity*
96	uses to seal *usually seals*
98	liver *The supposed seat of love and violent passion.*
103–4	The . . . altered *The metre is changed.*
106	brock *badger (contemptuous)*
108	Lucrece knife *Lucrece killed herself because her chastity was lost; Olivia, the letter implies, finds chaste silence just as killing.*
111	fustian *nonsensical, foolish*
112	wench *i.e. Maria*

FABIAN   Nay, patience, or we break the sinews of
our plot.

MALVOLIO   Besides, you waste the treasure of your   80
time with a foolish knight . . .

SIR ANDREW   That's me, I warrant you.

MALVOLIO   One Sir Andrew.

SIR ANDREW   I knew 'twas I, for many do call me fool.

MALVOLIO   [*Picking up the letter*] What employment
have we here?

FABIAN   Now is the woodcock near the gin.

SIR TOBY   O, peace, and the spirit of humours inti-
mate reading aloud to him!

MALVOLIO   By my life, this is my lady's hand. These be
her very C's, her U's and her T's; and thus makes she   90
her great P's. It is, in contempt of question, her hand.

SIR ANDREW   Her C's, her U's and her T's? Why that?

MALVOLIO   [*Reads*] *To the unknown beloved this, and
my good wishes.* Her very phrases! By your leave,
wax. Soft! and the impressure her Lucrece, with
which she uses to seal. 'Tis my lady! To whom
should this be?

FABIAN   This wins him, liver and all.

MALVOLIO   [*Reads*] *Jove knows I love;*
                        But who?   100
                   Lips do not move
                   No man must know.
'No man must know'! What follows? The numbers
altered! 'No man must know'! If this should be thee,
Malvolio!

SIR TOBY   Marry, hang thee, brock!

MALVOLIO   [*Reads*]
              I may command where I adore;
                   But silence, like a Lucrece knife,
              With bloodless stroke my heart doth gore;
                   M.O.A.I. doth sway my life.   110

FABIAN   A fustian riddle!

SIR TOBY   Excellent wench, say I!

115	dressed *prepared for*
116	staniel *An inferior hawk.*
	checks at *swerves to swoop upon (a hawking term)*
120	formal capacity *normal intelligence*
121	obstruction *difficulty*
122	position *arrangement*
124	make up *complete*
126–7	Sowter . . . fox *i.e. the hound will bay after the false scent even though the deceit is gross as a fox's smell.*
131	faults *breaks in the scent*
132–3	consonancy . . . sequel *consistency in what follows*
133	that . . . probation *that permits of investigation*
135	O *i.e. lamentation*
141	simulation *hidden significance(?)*
142	crush *force*
143	are *Plural attracted by* letters.
145	revolve *reflect. (Here Malvolio might* revolve *on his feet, and almost detect the eavesdroppers).*
	stars *fortune*
149	inure *accustom*

94

MALVOLIO 'M.O.A.I. doth sway my life.' Nay, but first let me see, let me see, let me see . . .

FABIAN What dish o'poison has she dressed him!

SIR TOBY And with what wing the staniel checks at it!

MALVOLIO 'I may command where I adore'. Why, she may command me. I serve her, she is my lady. Why, this is evident to any formal capacity. There is no obstruction in this. And the end: what should that alphabetical position portend? If I could make that resemble something in me? Softly, 'M.O.A.I.' . . .

SIR TOBY O, ay, make up that. He is now at a cold scent.

FABIAN Sowter will cry upon't for all this, though it be as rank as a fox.

MALVOLIO M . . . Malvolio! M! Why, that begins my name!

FABIAN Did not I say he would work it out? The cur is excellent at faults.

MALVOLIO M! But then there is no consonancy in the sequel that suffers under probation. A should follow, but O does.

FABIAN And O shall end, I hope.

SIR TOBY Ay, or I'll cudgel him and make him cry O.

MALVOLIO And then I comes behind.

FABIAN Ay, an you had any eye behind you, you might see more detraction at your heels than fortunes before you.

MALVOLIO M.O.A.I. This simulation is not as the former. And yet, to crush this a little, it would bow to me, for every one of these letters are in my name. Soft! Here follows prose. [*Reads*] *If this fall into thy hand, revolve. In my stars I am above thee, but be not afraid of greatness. Some are born great, some achieve greatness, and some have greatness thrust upon 'em. Thy fates open their hands, let thy blood and spirit embrace them; and to inure thyself to what thou art like*

120

130

140

95

150	cast *cast off*
	slough *skin (of a snake)*
150–1	opposite *hostile*
152	teng *ring with*
152–3	trick of singularity *affectation of eccentricity*

| 155 | cross-gartered *i.e. with garters below the knee that crossed at the back of the leg and fastened in a bow above the knee.* Yellow *stockings and* cross-gartering *were old-fashioned by 1600.* Yellow *was the colour of Narcissus (self-love).* |
| 156 | Go to *i.e. come on* |

161	champain discovers *open country reveals*
162	politic *political*
163	baffle *disgrace*
164	point-devise *extremely precise (adjective), or precisely (adverb)*
165	jade *deceive*
166	excites to *enforces*

169	injunction *A judicial process by which one who is threatening (e.g. Malvolio) to invade the rights of another is ordered to restore matters to the position in which they previously stood.*
170	habits *clothes*
171	strange *haughty*
	stout *proud*
173	putting on *the putting on of clothes; the assuming of a real or feigned character*
174	yet *still*
175	entertain'st *acceptest*
177	still *always*

| 181 | Sophy *Shah of Persia. An allusion to the Shah's bounty to two English brothers, Sir Robert and Sir Anthony Shirley, who visited Persia in 1599. Sir Robert helped to reorganise the Persian army (compare 'fencer to the Sophy', III. 4. 289–90). A pamphlet about the Shirleys was published in 1600.* |

to be, cast thy humble slough and appear fresh. Be oppo- 150
site with a kinsman, surly with servants. Let thy tongue
tang arguments of state. Put thyself into the trick of
singularity. She thus advises thee that sighs for thee.
Remember who commended thy yellow stockings and
wished to see thee ever cross-gartered. I say, remember.
Go to, thou art made if thou desir'st to be so. If not, let
me see thee a steward still, the fellow of servants, and
not worthy to touch Fortune's fingers. Farewell. She
that would alter services with thee, The Fortunate
Unhappy. 160

Daylight and champain discovers not more! This is
open. I will be proud, I will read politic authors, I
will baffle Sir Toby, I will wash off gross acquaintance, I will be point-devise, the very man. I do not
now fool myself, to let imagination jade me; for every
reason excites to this, that my lady loves me. She did
commend my yellow stockings of late, she did praise
my leg being cross-gartered; and in this she mani-
fests herself to my love and with a kind of injunction
drives me to these habits of her liking. I thank my 170
stars, I am happy! I will be stránge, stout, in yellow
stockings and cross-gartered, even with the swiftness
of putting on. Jove and my stars be praised! Here is
yet a postscript. [*Reads*] *Thou canst not choose but know
who I am. If thou entertain'st my love let it appear in thy
smiling, thy smiles become thee well. Therefore in my
presence still smile, dear my sweet, I prithee.* Jove, I
thank thee! I will smile. I will do everything that thou
wilt have me! [*Exit*

FABIAN   I will not give my part of this sport for a 180
pension of thousands to be paid from the Sophy.

SIR TOBY   I could marry this wench for this device.

SIR ANDREW So could I too.

SIR TOBY   And ask no other dowry with her but such
another jest.

                    Enter MARIA

187   gull-catcher *fool-catcher*

190   play *gamble for*
       tray-trip *A dice game, in which the winner had to throw
           threes.*

196   aqua-vitae *spirits*

204   contempt *disgrace, dishonour*
205   Tartar *Tartarus (hell)*

207   make one *be one of the party. Or does he mean that he
           hopes to be a* devil of wit *too?*

SIR ANDREW Nor I neither.

FABIAN Here comes my noble gull-catcher.

SIR TOBY Wilt thou set thy foot o'my neck?

SIR ANDREW Or o'mine either?

SIR TOBY Shall I play my freedom at tray-trip and 190
become thy bondslave?

SIR ANDREW I'faith, or I either?

SIR TOBY Why, thou hast put him in such a dream
that when the image of it leaves him he must run mad.

MARIA Nay, but say true: does it work upon him?

SIR TOBY Like aqua-vitae with a midwife.

MARIA If you will then see the fruits of the sport,
mark his first approach before my lady. He will come
to her in yellow stockings, and 'tis a colour she abhors; and cross-gartered, a fashion she detests; and 200
he will smile upon her, which will now be so unsuit-
able to her disposition, being addicted to a melancholy as she is, that it cannot but turn him into a
notable contempt. If you will see it, follow me.

SIR TOBY To the gates of Tartar, thou most excellent
devil of wit!

SIR ANDREW I'll make one too.

[*Exeunt*

tabor *small drum. The stage-clown traditionally played a tabor and a pipe, and Feste perhaps entertained the audience between the acts (if act-intervals were observed).*

1   Save *God save*

2   live by *make a living by*

3   by *near*

8   lies by *dwells near; goes to bed with*

10 tabor *A pun:* tabern = *tavern;* tabor *(drum). The word was probably slurred.*
    stand by *stands near; is upheld by*

12 cheveril *kid leather*

14 dally nicely *play subtly*

15 wanton *unmanageable. (Feste takes in the sense 'un-chaste').*

21-22 words . . . them *i.e. words have lost their standing ever since bonds have been required to back them (in business etc.)*

24 Troth *By my truth*

ACT THREE

Scene 1. Enter at different doors VIOLA, *and* FESTE *playing his pipe and tabor*

VIOLA   Save thee, friend, and thy music. Dost thou live by thy tabor?

FESTE   No, sir, I live by the church.

VIOLA   Art thou a Churchman?

FESTE   No such matter, sir; I do live by the church. For I do live at my house, and my house doth stand by the church.

VIOLA   So thou mayst say the king lies by a beggar, if a beggar dwell near him; or the church stands by thy tabor, if thy tabor stand by the church.   10

FESTE   You have said, sir. To see this age! A sentence is but a cheveril glove to a good wit; how quickly the wrong side may be turned outward!

VIOLA   Nay, that's certain. They that dally nicely with words may quickly make them wanton.

FESTE   I would therefore my sister had had no name, sir.

VIOLA   Why, man?

FESTE   Why, sir, her name's a word, and to dally with that word might make my sister wanton. But   20 indeed, words are very rascals, since bonds disgraced them.

VIOLA   Thy reason, man?

FESTE   Troth, sir, I can yield you none without words, and words are grown so false, I am loath to prove reason with them.

VIOLA   I warrant thou art a merry fellow, and car'st for nothing.

FESTE   Not so, sir. I do care for something; but in my conscience, sir, I do not care for you. If that be   30 to care for nothing, sir, I would it would make you invisible.

VIOLA   Art not thou the Lady Olivia's fool?

FESTE   No indeed, sir, the Lady Olivia has no
folly. She will keep no fool, sir, till she be married,
and fools are as like husbands as pilchers are to her-
rings; the husband's the bigger. I am indeed not her
fool, but her corrupter of words.

VIOLA   I saw thee late at the Count Orsino's.

FESTE   Foolery, sir, does walk about the orb like   40
the sun, it shines everywhere. I would be sorry, sir,
but the fool should be as oft with your master as with
my mistress. I think I saw your wisdom there.

VIOLA   Nay, an thou pass upon me, I'll no more
with thee. Hold, there's expenses for thee!

                    She gives him a coin

FESTE   Now Jove, in his next commodity of hair,
send thee a beard!

VIOLA   By my troth, I'll tell thee, I am almost
sick for one – [*Aside*] though I would not have it
grow on my chin. [*Aloud*] Is thy lady within?   50

FESTE   Would not a pair of these have bred, sir?

VIOLA   Yes, being kept together and put to use.

FESTE   I would play Lord Pandarus of Phrygia,
sir, to bring a Cressida to this Troilus.

VIOLA   I understand you, sir, 'tis well begged.

                    She gives another coin

FESTE   The matter, I hope, is not great, sir, begging but a beggar – Cressida was a beggar. My lady
is within, sir. I will conster to them whence you come.
Who you are and what you would are out of my welkin – I might say 'element', but the word is over-   60
worn.   [*Exit*

VIOLA   This fellow is wise enough to play the fool,
      And to do that well craves a kind of wit.
      He must observe their mood on whom he jests,
      The quality of persons, and the time,
      And, like the haggard, check at every feather
      That comes before his eye. This is a practice

69	fit *fitting*
70	folly-fall'n . . . wit *stooping to folly, impair their reputation for common sense*
73-4	Dieu . . . serviteur *God keep you, sir. — And you too; your servant. (French).*
76	encounter *approach. Toby derides ceremonious speech, but Viola gives as good as she gets.*
77	trade *business*
78	bound to *bound for (as a trader); obliged to*
79	list *destination*
80	Taste *Try*
81	understand *i.e. stand under, support*
85	answer *obey*
	gate and entrance *A pseudo-legal phrase?* Gate *(the right to pasturage for cattle on a piece of land) puns on* gait.
86	prevented *forestalled*
91	My . . . voice *My material (or subject) must not be uttered*
92	pregnant *ready, receptive*
	vouchsafed *graciously attentive*
94	ready *i.e. ready to use (by writing them in his pocket-book?)*

As full of labour as a wise man's art.
For folly that he wisely shows is fit;
But wise men, folly-fall'n, quite taint their wit.   70
Enter SIR TOBY *and* SIR ANDREW

SIR TOBY   Save you, gentleman!

VIOLA   And you, sir!

SIR ANDREW   *Dieu vous garde, monsieur!*

VIOLA   *Et vous aussi; votre serviteur!*

SIR ANDREW   I hope, sir, you are, and I am yours.

SIR TOBY   Will you encounter the house? My niece
is desirous you should enter, if your trade be to her.

VIOLA   I am bound to your niece, sir. I mean, she
is the list of my voyage.

SIR TOBY   Taste your legs, sir; put them to motion.   80

VIOLA   My legs do better understand me, sir, than
I understand what you mean by bidding me taste my
legs.

SIR TOBY   I mean to go, sir, to enter.

VIOLA   I will answer you with gate and entrance.
Enter OLIVIA *and* MARIA
But we are prevented. [*To* OLIVIA] Most excellent,
accomplished lady, the heavens rain odours on
you!

SIR ANDREW   [*Aside*] That youth's a rare courtier. 'Rain
odours'! Well!   90

VIOLA   My matter hath no voice, lady, but to your
own most pregnant and vouchsafed ear.

SIR ANDREW   'Odours', 'pregnant', and 'vouchsafed'!
I'll get 'em all three all ready.

OLIVIA   Let the garden door be shut and leave me
to my hearing.

[*Exeunt* SIR TOBY *and* MARIA
SIR ANDREW *lingers and then goes too*
Give me your hand, sir.

VIOLA   My duty, madam, and most humble service!

OLIVIA   What is your name?

101	'Twas . . . world *i.e. the world has changed for the worse*
102	lowly feigning *pretended humility*
	compliment *formal civility*
104	And . . . yours *The lover was his lady's 'servant'.*

| 106 | For *As for* |

113	music . . . spheres *Alluding to the notion, deriving from Ptolemaic astronomy, that the universe was constructed of crystalline spheres that produced music as they turned.*
115	Give . . . you *allow me to speak, I beseech you*
117	abuse *do violence to; insult; deceive*

| 119 | hard construction *harsh interpretation* |

| 121 | might *could* |

122	at the stake *A bear-baiting image.*
123	baited . . . thoughts *persecuted it with unrestrained thoughts (as a bear was attacked for sport with unmuzzled dogs)*
124	receiving *perception*
125	cypress *Crêpe-like fabric, or kerchief made of this, used for mourning (alluded to because transparent).*

| 127 | degree *step* |

106

VIOLA	Cesario is your servant's name, fair prin- cess.

OLIVIA	My servant, sir? 'Twas never merry world Since lowly feigning was called compliment. Y'are servant to the Count Orsino, youth.
VIOLA	And he is yours, and his must needs be yours. Your servant's servant is your servant, madam.
OLIVIA	For him, I think not on him. For his thoughts, Would they were blanks rather than filled with me.
VIOLA	Madam, I come to whet your gentle thoughts On his behalf –
OLIVIA	O, by your leave, I pray you. I bade you never speak again of him.

But would you undertake another suit,
I had rather hear you to solicit that
Than music from the spheres.

VIOLA	Dear lady –
OLIVIA	Give me leave, beseech you. I did send, After the last enchantment you did here, A ring in chase of you. So did I abuse Myself, my servant, and, I fear me, you. Under your hard construction must I sit, To force that on you in a shameful cunning

Which you knew none of yours. What might you
think?
Have you not set mine honour at the stake
And baited it with all th'unmuzzled thoughts
That tyrannous heart can think? To one of your
receiving
Enough is shown; a cypress, not a bosom,
Hides my heart. So, let me hear you speak.

VIOLA	I pity you.
OLIVIA	That's a degree to love.

grize *step*
vulgar proof *everyday experience*

131   proud *referring to Cesario, or to herself?*

136   harvest *maturity*
137   proper *capital; handsome*
138   due west *i.e. she dismisses him, hinting that he has a long*
        way to go before his sun will set
      westward ho! *The cry of the Thames watermen.*
139   good disposition *i.e. tranquillity of mind*
140   You'll *You'll send*

143   That . . . are *i.e. that you forget yourself*

144   I . . . you *i.e. because she thinks Cesario a nobleman in*
        disguise

148   your fool *i.e. you are making a fool of me*

152   love's . . . noon *i.e. love cannot be hidden*

155   maugre *despite*

157-8 Do . . . cause *Do not force yourself to think that, because*
        I woo, you have no business to woo me. For that =
        because.

108

VIOLA   No, not a grize; for 'tis a vulgar proof
             That very oft we pity enemies.

OLIVIA   Why, then, methinks 'tis time to smile
                 again.   130
             O world, how apt the poor are to be proud!
             If one should be a prey, how much the better
             To fall before the lion than the wolf!
                      A clock strikes
             The clock upbraids me with the waste of time.
             Be not afraid, good youth; I will not have you.
             And yet, when wit and youth is come to harvest,
             Your wife is like to reap a proper man.
             There lies your way, due west.

VIOLA   Then westward ho!
             Grace and good disposition attend your ladyship.
             You'll nothing, madam, to my lord by me?   140

OLIVIA   Stay!
             I prithee, tell me what thou think'st of me?

VIOLA   That you do think you are not what you
                 are.

OLIVIA   If I think so, I think the same of you.

VIOLA   Then think you right; I am not what I am.

OLIVIA   I would you were as I would have you be.

VIOLA   Would it be better, madam, than I am?
             I wish it might, for now I am your fool.

OLIVIA   [*Aside*] O, what a deal of scorn looks
                 beautiful
             In the contempt and anger of his lip!   150
             A murd'rous guilt shows not itself more soon
             Than love that would seem hid; love's night is
                 noon.
             [*To* VIOLA] Cesario, by the roses of the spring,
             By maidhood, honour, truth, and everything,
             I love thee so that, maugre all thy pride,
             Nor wit nor reason can my passion hide.
             Do not extort thy reasons from this clause –
             For that I woo thou therefore hast no cause.

ACT THREE, scene 2

But rather reason thus with reason fetter –
Love sought, is good; but given unsought, is
better.   160

VIOLA   By innocence I swear, and by my youth,
I have one heart, one bosom, and one truth.
And that no woman has, nor never none
Shall mistress be of it, save I alone.
And so adieu, good madam; never more
Will I my master's tears to you deplore.

OLIVIA   Yet come again; for thou perhaps mayst
move
That heart, which now abhors, to like his love.

[*Exeunt*

Scene 2. *Enter* SIR TOBY, SIR ANDREW, *and* FABIAN

SIR ANDREW No, faith, I'll not stay a jot longer.

SIR TOBY   Thy reason, dear venom, give thy reason.

FABIAN   You must needs yield your reason, Sir
Andrew.

SIR ANDREW Marry, I saw your niece do more favours
to the Count's servingman than ever she bestowed
upon me. I saw't i'th'orchard.

SIR TOBY   Did she see thee the while, old boy, tell me
that?

SIR ANDREW As plain as I see you now.   10

FABIAN   This was a great argument of love in her
toward you.

SIR ANDREW 'Slight! Will you make an ass o'me?

FABIAN   I will prove it legitimate, sir, upon the
oaths of judgement and reason.

SIR TOBY   And they have been grand-jury men since
before Noah was a sailor.

FABIAN   She did show favour to the youth in your
sight only to exasperate you, to awake your dormouse
valour, to put fire in your heart and brimstone in your   20
liver. You should then have accosted her, and with

some excellent jests fire-new from the mint, you should have banged the youth into dumbness. This was looked for at your hand, and this was baulked. The double gilt of this opportunity you let time wash off, and you are now sailed into the north of my lady's opinion; where you will hang like an icicle on a Dutchman's beard, unless you do redeem it by some laudable attempt either of valour or policy.

SIR ANDREW An't be any way, it must be with valour, 30 for policy I hate. I had as lief be a Brownist as a politician.

SIR TOBY   Why then, build me thy fortunes upon the basis of valour. Challenge me the Count's youth to fight with him; hurt him in eleven places; my niece shall take note of it; and assure thyself, there is no love-broker in the world can more prevail in man's commendation with woman than report of valour.

FABIAN   There is no way but this, Sir Andrew.

SIR ANDREW Will either of you bear me a challenge to 40 him?

SIR TOBY   Go, write it in a martial hand. Be curst and brief. It is no matter how witty, so it be eloquent and full of invention. Taunt him with the licence of ink. If thou thou'st him some thrice it shall not be amiss, and as many lies as will lie in thy sheet of paper – although the sheet were big enough for the bed of Ware in England, set 'em down, go, about it. Let there be gall enough in thy ink, though thou write with a goose pen, no matter. About it!   50

SIR ANDREW Where shall I find you?

SIR TOBY   We'll call thee at the cubiculo. Go!

[*Exit* SIR ANDREW

FABIAN   This is a dear manikin to you, Sir Toby.

SIR TOBY   I have been dear to him, lad, some two thousand strong or so.

FABIAN   We shall have a rare letter from him – but you'll not deliver't.

113

ACT THREE, scene 3

SIR TOBY   Never trust me then – and by all means stir on the youth to an answer. I think oxen and wain-ropes cannot hale them together. For Andrew, if he were opened and you find so much blood in his liver as will clog the foot of a flea, I'll eat the rest of th'anatomy. 60

FABIAN   And his opposite the youth bears in his visage no great presage of cruelty.

Enter MARIA

SIR TOBY   Look where the youngest wren of nine comes.

MARIA   If you desire the spleen, and will laugh yourselves into stitches, follow me. Yond gull Mal-volio is turned heathen, a very renegado; for there is no Christian, that means to be saved by believing rightly, can ever believe such impossible passages of grossness. He's in yellow stockings! 70

SIR TOBY   And cross-gartered?

MARIA   Most villainously; like a pedant that keeps a school i'th'church. I have dogged him like his mur-derer. He does obey every point of the letter that I dropped to betray him. He does smile his face into more lines than is in the new map with the augmen-tation of the Indies. You have not seen such a thing as 'tis. I can hardly forbear hurling things at him – I know my lady will strike him. If she do, he'll smile, and take't for a great favour. 80

SIR TOBY   Come, bring us, bring us where he is.

[*Exeunt*

Scene 3. *Enter* SEBASTIAN *and* ANTONIO

SEBASTIAN   I would not by my will have troubled you,
But since you make your pleasure of your pains
I will no further chide you.

ANTONIO   I could not stay behind you. My desire
More sharp than filèd steel, did spur me forth,
And not all love to see you – though so much

8   jealousy *anxiety*

9   skilless in *unacquainted with*

12   The rather *The more readily*

16   shuffled off *got rid of evasively, i.e. not properly repaid*
       uncurrent *worthless*

17   worth *means*
       conscience *consciousness (of my debt)*

19   reliques *antiquities, monuments*

24   pardon *excuse*

26   Count his *Count's*

28   it . . . answered *it would be difficult to make out a defence*

29   Belike *I suppose*

31   quality *nature*

32   argument *debate*

33   answered *compensated*

34   traffic's *trade's*

35   myself stood out *I myself refused to join the others, held out*

36   lapsèd *apprehended*

116

As might have drawn one to a longer voyage –
But jealousy what might befall your travel,
Being skilless in these parts; which to a stranger,
Unguided and unfriended, often prove   10
Rough and unhospitable. My willing love
The rather by these arguments of fear
Set forth in your pursuit.

SEBASTIAN   My kind Antonio,
I can no other answer make but thanks,
And thanks, and ever thanks; and oft good turns
Are shuffled off with such uncurrent pay.
But were my worth, as is my conscience, firm,
You should find better dealing. What's to do?
Shall we go see the reliques of this town?

ANTONIO   Tomorrow, sir; best first go see your
lodging.   20

SEBASTIAN   I am not weary, and 'tis long to night.
I pray you, let us satisfy our eyes
With the memorials and the things of fame
That do renown this city.

ANTONIO   Would you'd pardon me.
I do not without danger walk these streets.
Once in a sea-fight 'gainst the Count his galleys
I did some service – of such note indeed
That, were I ta'en here, it would scarce be
answered.

SEBASTIAN   Belike you slew great number of his people?

ANTONIO   Th'offence is not of such a bloody nature,   30
Albeit the quality of the time and quarrel
Might well have given us bloody argument.
It might have since been answered in repaying
What we took from them, which, for traffic's
sake,
Most of our city did. Only myself stood out,
For which, if I be lapsèd in this place,
I shall pay dear.

SEBASTIAN   Do not then walk too open.

ACT THREE, scene 4

ANTONIO   It doth not fit me. Hold, sir, here's my
              purse.
            In the south suburbs, at the Elephant,
            Is best to lodge. I will bespeak our diet   40
            Whiles you beguile the time, and feed your
              knowledge
            With viewing of the town. There shall you have
              me.
SEBASTIAN   Why I your purse?
ANTONIO   Haply your eye shall light upon some toy
            You have desire to purchase; and your store,
            I think, is not for idle markets, sir.
SEBASTIAN   I'll be your purse-bearer, and leave you for
            An hour.
ANTONIO   To th'Elephant.
SEBASTIAN   I do remember.   50

                                    [*Exeunt separately*

Scene 4. *Enter* OLIVIA *and* MARIA

OLIVIA   [*Aside*] I have sent after him, he says he'll
              come.
            How shall I feast him? What bestow of him?
            For youth is bought more oft than begged or
              borrowed.
            I speak too loud.
            [*To* MARIA] Where's Malvolio? He is sad and
              civil,
            And suits well for a servant with my fortunes.
            Where is Malvolio?
MARIA   He's coming, madam, but in very strange
            manner. He is sure possessed, madam.
OLIVIA   Why, what's the matter? Does he rave?   10
MARIA   No, madam, he does nothing but smile.
            Your ladyship were best to have some guard about
            you if he come, for sure the man is tainted in's wits.

16   sad *serious*

24   sonnet *song*
        Please . . . all *The refrain of a popular song*

28   black . . . yellow *Both colours suggested melancholy.*
29   It *i.e. Maria's letter*
30–1   sweet . . . hand *Elegant Roman or Italian style of
            writing (which was beginning to replace the older
            English style).*

33–4   Ay . . . thee *A line from a popular song.*

38–9   At . . . daws (*Should I answer*) *at your request? Yes,
            since nightingales answer jackdaws.*
40–1   boldness *Maria cleverly leads him to the ideas expressed
            in her letter.*

OLIVIA   Go, call him hither.

[*Exit* MARIA

I am as mad as he
If sad and merry madness equal be.

Enter MALVOLIO *and* MARIA

How now, Malvolio?

MALVOLIO   Sweet lady, ho, ho!

OLIVIA   Smil'st thou? I sent for thee upon a sad
occasion.   20

MALVOLIO   Sad, lady? I could be sad. This does make
some obstruction in the blood, this cross-gartering –
but what of that? If it please the eye of one, it is with
me as the very true sonnet is: 'Please one and please
all'.

OLIVIA   Why, how dost thou, man? What is the
matter with thee?

MALVOLIO   Not black in my mind, though yellow in
my legs. It did come to his hands, and commands
shall be executed. I think we do know the sweet   30
Roman hand.

OLIVIA   Wilt thou go to bed, Malvolio?

MALVOLIO   To bed! 'Ay, sweetheart, and I'll come to
thee!'

OLIVIA   God comfort thee! Why dost thou smile
so, and kiss thy hand so oft?

MARIA   How do you, Malvolio?

MALVOLIO   At your request? Yes; nightingales answer
daws.

MARIA   Why appear you with this ridiculous bold-   40
ness before my lady?

MALVOLIO   'Be not afraid of greatness.' 'Twas well
writ.

OLIVIA   What mean'st thou by that, Malvolio?

MALVOLIO   'Some are born great –'

OLIVIA   Ha?

MALVOLIO   'Some achieve greatness –'

OLIVIA   What sayst thou?

52   thy *Part of the humour of the scene, now lost, consists in Malvolio's use of the familiar 'thou' to his mistress.*

61   midsummer madness *A proverbial phrase. Great heat was believed to induce odd behaviour and madness.*

63   hardly *with difficulty*

68   miscarry *come to harm*

70   come near me *begin to understand who I am*

73   stubborn *rough*

79   reverend carriage *dignified bodily deportment*
79–80   in . . . note *in the way of dressing of some eminent personage*
80   limed *caught (as birds are caught with bird-lime)*
82   fellow *The customary title of address to a servant. But Malvolio takes it as 'this my equal'.*

122

MALVOLIO	'And some have greatness thrust upon them.'
OLIVIA	Heaven restore thee!
MALVOLIO	'Remember who commended thy yellow stockings –'
OLIVIA	Thy yellow stockings?
MALVOLIO	'– and wished to see thee cross-gartered.'
OLIVIA	Cross-gartered?
MALVOLIO	'Go to, thou art made if thou desir'st to be so.'
OLIVIA	Am I made?
MALVOLIO	'If not, let me see thee a servant still.'
OLIVIA	Why, this is very midsummer madness.

Enter a SERVANT

SERVANT   Madam, the young gentleman of the Count Orsino's is returned. I could hardly entreat him back. He attends your ladyship's pleasure.

OLIVIA   I'll come to him.   [*Exit* SERVANT
Good Maria, let this fellow be looked to. Where's my cousin Toby? Let some of my people have a special care of him. I would not have him miscarry for the half of my dowry.

[*Exeunt* OLIVIA *and* MARIA

MALVOLIO   O ho! Do you come near me now? No worse man than Sir Toby to look to me! This concurs directly with the letter. She sends him on purpose, that I may appear stubborn to him; for she incites me to that in the letter. 'Cast thy humble slough,' says she. 'Be opposite with a kinsman, surly with servants. let thy tongue tang with arguments of state. put thyself into the trick of singularity' – and consequently sets down the manner how: as a sad face, a reverend carriage, a slow tongue, in the habit of some sir of note, and so forth. I have limed her! But it is Jove's doing, and Jove make me thankful! And when she went away now – 'let this fellow be looked to'. Fellow! Not 'Malvolio', nor after my

83-4	after . . . degree *according to my position (in the house-* *hold)*
85	dram *apothecary's weight for 1/8 oz.; very small* *quantity*
	scruple *apothecary's weight for 1/3 dram; doubt. That* *is, 'no particle of doubt'.*
86	incredulous *incredible*
	unsafe *doubtful*
92	drawn . . . little *contracted into (Malvolio's) little size*
	Legion *The spirit that possessed a madman, described in* *Mark V. 9, Luke VIII. 30.*
97	private *privacy*
102	Go to *Come along (a vague remonstrance)*
103	Let . . . alone *Let me deal with him*
109	Carry . . . woman *i.e for analysis*
116	move *upset*
119	rough *violent*
124	

degree, but 'fellow'! Why, everything adheres together, that no dram of a scruple, no scruple of a scruple, no obstacle, no incredulous or unsafe circumstance – what can be said? – nothing that can be, can come between me and the full prospect of my hopes. Well, Jove, not I, is the doer of this, and he is to be thanked.   90

Enter SIR TOBY, FABIAN, *and* MARIA

SIR TOBY   Which way is he, in the name of sanctity? If all the devils of hell be drawn in little and Legion himself possessed him, yet I'll speak to him.

FABIAN   Here he is, here he is. How is't with you, sir? How is't with you, man?

MALVOLIO   Go off, I discard you. Let me enjoy my private. Go off!

MARIA   Lo, how hollow the fiend speaks within him! Did not I tell you? Sir Toby, my lady prays you to have a care of him.   100

MALVOLIO   Ah ha! Does she so!

SIR TOBY   Go to, go to! Peace, peace, we must deal gently with him. Let me alone. How do you, Malvolio? How is't with you? What, man, defy the devil! Consider, he's an enemy to mankind.

MALVOLIO   Do you know what you say?

MARIA   La you, an you speak ill of the devil, how he takes it at heart! Pray God he be not bewitched!

FABIAN   Carry his water to th'wise woman.

MARIA   Marry, and it shall be done tomorrow 110 morning, if I live. My lady would not lose him, for more than I'll say.

MALVOLIO   How now, mistress?

MARIA   O Lord!

SIR TOBY   Prithee, hold thy peace, this is not the way. Do you not see you move him? Let me alone with him.

FABIAN   No way but gentleness, gently, gently. The fiend is rough, and will not be roughly used.

120	bawcock *fine fellow (French* beau coq)
121	chuck *chick*
123	biddy *chickabiddy. Toby may be singing a line from a lost song, or he may be clucking encouragingly at Malvolio.*
124	cherry-pit *A children's game played with cherry-stones.*
125	collier *coal-vendor*
131	idle *trifling*
132	element *sphere of life*
135	If . . . now *Compare* Julius Caesar, *III. 1. 111–16, or* The Winter's Tale, *V. 2. 28 ff., for the pretence that 'we are not in the theatre'.*
137–8	His . . . device *i.e. his very soul has been poisoned by the trick*
139–40	take . . . taint *be exposed and spoilt. Fresh air was thought dangerous for the 'infected' or sick.*
143–4	in . . . bound *The usual treatment for madmen.*
145	carry it *i.e. carry it off*
148	to the bar *Perhaps 'to the open, to the bar (tribunal) of public opinion', as in* Richard III, *V. 3. 198–9: 'All several sins . . . Throng to the bar, crying all "Guilty! guilty!"'*
148–9	a . . . madmen *one of a jury appointed to find out if an accused person is insane(?)*
150	May morning *i.e. May-game or pageant*
153	saucy *Note the pun.*

SIR TOBY   Why, how now, my bawcock? How dost 120
thou, chuck?

MALVOLIO   Sir!

SIR TOBY   Ay, biddy, come with me. What, man, 'tis
not for gravity to play at cherry-pit with Satan. Hang
him, foul collier!

MARIA   Get him to say his prayers, good Sir Toby;
get him to pray.

MALVOLIO   My prayers, minx!

MARIA   No, I warrant you, he will not hear of
godliness.   130

MALVOLIO   Go, hang yourselves all. You are idle,
shallow things; I am not of your element. You shall
know more hereafter.   [*Exit*

SIR TOBY   Is't possible?

FABIAN   If this were played upon a stage now, I
could condemn it as an improbable fiction.

SIR TOBY   His very genius hath taken the infection of
the device, man.

MARIA   Nay, pursue him now, lest the device take
air, and taint.   140

FABIAN   Why, we shall make him mad indeed.

MARIA   The house will be the quieter.

SIR TOBY   Come, we'll have him in a dark room and
bound. My niece is already in the belief that he's mad.
We may carry it thus for our pleasure and his
penance till our very pastime, tired out of breath,
prompt us to have mercy on him; at which time, we
will bring the device to the bar, and crown thee for a
finder of madmen. But see, but see!

Enter SIR ANDREW

FABIAN   More matter for a May morning!   150

SIR ANDREW   Here's the challenge, read it. I warrant
there's vinegar and pepper in't.

FABIAN   Is't so saucy?

SIR ANDREW   Ay, is't, I warrant him. Do but read.

127

158   admire *marvel*

169   chance *good fortune*

173   windy side *safe side*
         the law *Fabian refers to the* criminal *law, while Andrew
           was thinking of the law of the duello and its cere-
           monies (for which see* As You Like It, *V. 4. 67–100).*

177   hope *i.e. of winning. But he seems to say that he hopes for
         something better than salvation!*
178   as . . . him *as thy usage of him deserves*

182   commerce *conversation*

184   Scout me for *Look out for*
185   bum-baily *bailiff (who arrested debtors)*

189   approbation *confirmation*
         proof *actual trial*
191   let . . . swearing *leave it to me to swear effectively*

128

SIR TOBY   Give me. [*Reads*] *Youth, whatsoever thou art, thou art but a scurvy fellow.*

FABIAN   Good and valiant.

SIR TOBY   [*Reads*] *Wonder not, nor admire not in thy mind why I do call thee so, for I will show thee no reason for't.*   160

FABIAN   A good note, that keeps you from the blow of the law.

SIR TOBY   [*Reads*] *Thou com'st to the Lady Olivia, and in my sight she uses thee kindly. But thou liest in thy throat; that is not the matter I challenge thee for.*

FABIAN   Very brief, and to exceeding good sense – [*Aside*] less!

SIR TOBY   [*Reads*] *I will waylay thee going home; where, if it be thy chance to kill me –*

FABIAN   Good!   170

SIR TOBY   [*Reads*] *thou kill'st me like a rogue and a villain.*

FABIAN   Still you keep o'th' windy side of the law; good.

SIR TOBY   [*Reads*] *Fare thee well, and God have mercy upon one of our souls. He may have mercy upon mine, but my hope is better – and so, look to thyself. Thy friend as thou usest him, and thy sworn enemy, Andrew Aguecheek.* If this letter move him not, his legs cannot. I'll give't him.   180

MARIA   You may have very fit occasion for't. He is now in some commerce with my lady, and will by and by depart.

SIR TOBY   Go, Sir Andrew. Scout me for him at the corner of the orchard like a bum-baily. So soon as ever thou seest him, draw, and as thou draw'st, swear horrible; for it comes to pass oft that a terrible oath, with a swaggering accent sharply twanged off, gives manhood more approbation than ever proof itself would have earned him. Away!   190

SIR ANDREW   Nay, let me alone for swearing.   [*Exit*

198	clodpole *blockhead*
199–200	set . . . valour *give Aguecheek a notable reputation for courage*
204	cockatrices *fabulous monsters able to kill with a glance*
205–6	Give . . . way *Keep out of their way*
206	presently *immediately*
207	horrid *terrifying*
210	And . . . on't *And staked (wagered) my honour too carelessly upon it (your heart). Some editors emend on't to* out.
214	'haviour *behaviour, manner*
216	jewel *jewelled miniature*
220	That . . . give *that honour may grant, when requested, without compromising itself*

SIR TOBY   Now will not I deliver his letter. For the
behaviour of the young gentleman gives him out to
be of good capacity and breeding; his employment
between his lord and my niece confirms no less.
Therefore this letter, being so excellently ignorant,
will breed no terror in the youth; he will find it comes
from a clodpole. But, sir, I will deliver his challenge
by word of mouth, set upon Aguecheek a notable
report of valour, and drive the gentleman – as I know 200
his youth will aptly receive it – into a most hideous
opinion of his rage, skill, fury, and impetuosity. This
will so fright them both that they will kill one
another by the look, like cockatrices.

                Enter OLIVIA *and* VIOLA

FABIAN   Here he comes with your niece. Give them
way till he take leave, and presently after him.

SIR TOBY   I will meditate the while upon some horrid
message for a challenge.

                [*Exeunt* SIR TOBY, FABIAN, *and* MARIA

OLIVIA   I have said too much unto a heart of stone,
          And laid mine honour too unchary on't.   210
          There's something in me that reproves my fault.
          But such a headstrong, potent fault it is,
          That it but mocks reproof.

VIOLA   With the same 'haviour that your passion
                                                bears
          Goes on my master's griefs.

OLIVIA   Here, wear this jewel for me, 'tis my
                                          picture.
          Refuse it not, it hath no tongue to vex you.
          And, I beseech you, come again tomorrow.
          What shall you ask of me that I'll deny
          That honour saved may upon asking give?   220

VIOLA   Nothing but this: your true love for my
                                            master.

OLIVIA   How with mine honour may I give him
                                            that

                                                    131

225   like thee *i.e. with your attractions*

226   thee *Not very courteous to a comparative stranger!*
        Viola replies with you.

230   despite *defiance*
231   attends *awaits*
231–2   Dismount . . . tuck *Draw your rapier*
232   yare *swift, prompt*

238   price *value*
239   opposite *adversary*

241   withal *with*

243   dubbed *created, made*
        unhatched *unhacked; or perhaps 'undrawn'*
244   on . . consideration *i.e. not for military service but*
        through (?financial) courtly connections

248   Hob, nob (*from* hab, nab) *have, have not, i.e. 'come*
        what may'
        word *motto*

251   conduct *escort, guard*

253   taste *test*
254   quirk *peculiarity*

Which I have given to you?

VIOLA   I will acquit you.

OLIVIA   Well, come again tomorrow. Fare thee
                well.
            A fiend like thee might bear my soul to hell.

                                                    [*Exit*

Enter SIR TOBY *and* FABIAN

SIR TOBY   Gentleman, God save thee!

VIOLA   And you, sir.

SIR TOBY   That defence thou hast, betake thee to't.
Of what nature the wrongs are thou hast done him, I
know not; but thy intercepter, full of despite, bloody   230
as the hunter, attends thee at the orchard end. Dismount thy tuck, be yare in thy preparation, for thy
assailant is quick, skilful and deadly.

VIOLA   You mistake, sir, I am sure. No man hath
any quarrel to me. My remembrance is very free and
clear from any image of offence done to any man.

SIR TOBY   You'll find it otherwise, I assure you.
Therefore, if you hold your life at any price, betake
you to your guard; for your opposite hath in him
what youth, strength, skill, and wrath can furnish   240
man withal.

VIOLA   I pray you, sir, what is he?

SIR TOBY   He is knight dubbed with unhatched
rapier and on carpet consideration – but he is a devil
in private brawl. Souls and bodies hath he divorced
three; and his incensement at this moment is so im-
placable, that satisfaction can be none, but by pangs
of death, and sepulchre. Hob, nob! is his word:
give't or take't.

VIOLA   I will return again into the house and   250
desire some conduct of the lady. I am no fighter. I
have heard of some kind of men that put quarrels
purposely on others to taste their valour. Belike this
is a man of that quirk.

SIR TOBY   Sir, no. His indignation derives itself out

256   competent *sufficient* ·

259   answer him *satisfy him in*
260   meddle *mingle in fight, engage in conflict*
261   forswear *renounce (the wearing of a sword, the mark of a
            gentleman)*
       iron *Cant for ' sword'*.

264   know *enquire*

266   nothing . . . purpose *not an intentional injury*

271   mortal arbitrement *decision by mortal combat*
271–2   circumstance *details*

275   form *appearance*

279   walk towards him *In Folio Viola and Fabian exeunt
            after l. 283 and re-enter after* ride you *(l. 301).*

282   Sir Priest *Sir = Latin* dominus, *the title of a graduate,
            therefore of a clergyman.*

285   firago *virago, warrior (of either sex in Shakespeare's
            time)*
       pass *bout*
286   stuck-in *thrust*
287   mortal motion *deadly movement*
       inevitable *inescapable*
287–8   on . . . you *after your return-blow he pays you home*
290   Sophy *Shah (compare II. 5. 181, note)*

of a very competent injury. Therefore, get you on and
give him his desire. Back you shall not to the house,
unless you undertake that with me, which with as
much safety you might answer him. Therefore on,
or strip your sword stark naked; for meddle you 260
must, that's certain, or forswear to wear iron about
you.

VIOLA   This is as uncivil as strange. I beseech you,
do me this courteous office, as to know of the knight
what my offence to him is. It is something of my
negligence, nothing of my purpose.

SIR TOBY   I will do so. Signor Fabian, stay you by
this gentleman till my return.   [*Exit*

VIOLA   Pray you, sir, do you know of this matter?

FABIAN   I know the knight is incensed against you, 270
even to a mortal arbitrement, but nothing of the circumstance more.

VIOLA   I beseech you, what manner of man is he?

FABIAN   Nothing of that wonderful promise, to
read him by his form, as you are like to find him in
the proof of his valour. He is indeed, sir, the most
skilful, bloody, and fatal opposite that you could
possibly have found in any part of Illyria. Will you
walk towards him? I will make your peace with him,
if I can.   280

VIOLA   I shall be much bound to you for't. I am
one that had rather go with Sir Priest than Sir
Knight; I care not who knows so much of my mettle.

            Enter SIR TOBY *and* SIR ANDREW

SIR TOBY   Why, man, he's a very devil. I have not
seen such a firago. I had a pass with him, rapier,
scabbard and all; and he gives me the stuck-in with
such a mortal motion that it is inevitable; and on the
answer, he pays you as surely as your feet hits the
ground they step on. They say he has been fencer
to the Sophy.   290

SIR ANDREW Pox on't! I'll not meddle with him.

SIR TOBY   Ay, but he will not now be pacified. Fabian
can scarce hold him yonder.

SIR ANDREW Plague on't! An I thought he had been
valiant, and so cunning in fence, I'd have seen him
damned ere I'd have challenged him. Let him let the
matter slip, and I'll give him my horse, grey Capilet.

SIR TOBY   I'll make the motion. Stand here, make a
good show on't. This shall end without the perdition
of souls. [*Aside, as he crosses to* FABIAN] Marry, I'll   300
ride your horse as well as I ride you! [*To* FABIAN] I
have his horse to take up the quarrel. I have persuaded him the youth's a devil.

FABIAN   He is as horribly conceited of him, and
pants and looks pale as if a bear were at his heels.

SIR TOBY   [*To* VIOLA] There's no remedy, sir, he will
fight with you for's oath's sake. Marry, he hath better
bethought him of his quarrel, and he finds that now
scarce to be worth talking of. Therefore, draw for the
supportance of his vow. He protests he will not hurt   310
you.

VIOLA   [*Aside*] Pray God defend me! A little thing
would make me tell them how much I lack of a man.

FABIAN   Give ground if you see him furious.

SIR TOBY   [*Crossing to* SIR ANDREW] Come, Sir
Andrew, there's no remedy. The gentleman will, for
his honour's sake, have one bout with you, he cannot by the *duello* avoid it. But he has promised me,
as he is a gentleman and a soldier, he will not hurt
you. Come on, to't!   320

SIR ANDREW Pray God he keep his oath!

He draws

Enter ANTONIO

VIOLA   I do assure you, 'tis against my will.

She draws

ANTONIO   [*To* SIR ANDREW] Put up your sword. If
this young gentleman
Have done offence, I take the fault on me.

137

329   undertaker *a helper; one who acts as surety or security for another; one who takes up a challenge(?)*

332   anon *soon*

335   for that *as for what*

338   office *duty*

341   favour *face*

345   answer *pay for, atone for; defend myself (against the accusation)*

349   amazed *bewildered*
350   be . . . comfort *be comforted*

355   part *partly*

356   ability *means*
357   having *wealth*

138

If you offend him, I for him defy you.

SIR TOBY   You, sir? Why, what are you?

ANTONIO   One, sir, that for his love dares yet do more
Than you have heard him brag to you he will.

SIR TOBY   Nay, if you be an undertaker, I am for you.

Enter two OFFICERS

FABIAN   O good Sir Toby, hold! Here come the 330
Officers.

SIR TOBY   [*To* ANTONIO] I'll be with you anon.

VIOLA   [*To* SIR ANDREW] Pray sir, put your sword
up, if you please.

SIR ANDREW Marry, will I, sir. And for that I promised
you, I'll be as good as my word. He will bear you
easily, and reins well.

FIRST OFFICER This is the man; do thy office.

SECOND OFFICER Antonio, I arrest thee at the suit
Of Count Orsino.

ANTONIO   You do mistake me, sir.   340

FIRST OFFICER No, sir, no jot. I know your favour well,
Though now you have no sea-cap on your head.
Take him away; he knows I know him well.

ANTONIO   I must obey. [*To* VIOLA] This comes with
seeking you.
But there's no remedy, I shall answer it.
What will you do, now my necessity
Makes me to ask you for my purse? It grieves me
Much more for what I cannot do for you
Than what befalls myself. You stand amazed;
But be of comfort.   350

SECOND OFFICER Come, sir, away!

ANTONIO   I must entreat of you some of that money.

VIOLA   What money, sir?
For the fair kindness you have showed me here,
And part being prompted by your present
trouble,
Out of my lean and low ability
I'll lend you something. My having is not much.

358	present *present resources*
359	coffer *resources*
361–2	my . . . persuasion *my claims upon you can fail to move you*
363	unsound *weak*
368	vainness *boasting*
374	sanctity . . . love *holy (devoted) love. The religious phrases here and in Antonio's next speech reflect the close connection (which goes back to mediaeval literature) between the language of Courtly Love and of Christianity.*
376	venerable *worthy of veneration*
378	vild *vile*
379	feature *appearance*
380–1	In . . . unkind *There is no real blemish in nature except in the mind; only those who are unnatural (unkind) in their minds can be called deformed*
383	trunks *chests, bodies*
	o'er-flourished *richly decorated (to conceal what is within)*

I'll make division of my present with you.
Hold: there's half my coffer.

ANTONIO   Will you deny me now?   360
Is't possible that my deserts to you
Can lack persuasion? Do not tempt my misery,
Lest that it make me so unsound a man
As to upbraid you with those kindnesses
That I have done for you.

VIOLA   I know of none.
Nor know I you by voice or any feature.
I hate ingratitude more in a man
Than lying, vainness, babbling drunkenness,
Or any taint of vice whose strong corruption
Inhabits our frail blood –

ANTONIO   O heavens themselves!   370

SECOND OFFICER Come, sir, I pray you go.

ANTONIO   Let me speak a little. This youth that you
                see here
I snatched one half out of the jaws of death;
Relieved him with such sanctity of love,
And to his image, which methought did promise
Most venerable worth, did I devotion!

FIRST OFFICER What's that to us? The time goes by.
                Away!

ANTONIO   But O, how vild an idol proves this god!
Thou hast, Sebastian, done good feature shame.
In nature there's no blemish but the mind,   380
None can be called deformed but the unkind.
Virtue is beauty; but the beauteous evil
Are empty trunks o'er-flourished by the devil.

FIRST OFFICER The man grows mad; away with him.
                Come, come, sir.

ANTONIO   Lead me on.
                        [*Exeunt* ANTONIO *and* OFFICERS

VIOLA   [*Aside*] Methinks his words do from such
                passion fly
That he believes himself. So! do not I?

392	sage saws *wise maxims*
393–4	I . . . glass *i.e. I know my brother to be so like me that whenever I look in my mirror he still seems alive*
395	favour *appearance; face*
396	Still *Always*
397	prove *prove true*
399	dishonest *dishonourable*
403	devout *zealous*
403–4	religious in it *i.e. behaving as if it were a principle of faith (to be a coward)*
405	'Slid *By God's eye-lid (mild oath)*
409	event *outcome*
410	yet *after all*

Prove true, imagination, O, prove true –
That I, dear brother, be now ta'en for you!

SIR TOBY   Come hither, knight; come hither, Fabian. 390
We'll whisper o'er a couplet or two of most sage
saws.

VIOLA   He named Sebastian. I my brother know
Yet living in my glass. Even such and so
In favour was my brother; and he went
Still in this fashion, colour, ornament,
For him I imitate. O, if it prove,
Tempests are kind, and salt waves fresh in love!
                                    [*Exit*

SIR TOBY   A very dishonest, paltry boy, and more a
coward than a hare. His dishonesty appears in leav- 400
ing his friend here in necessity and denying him; and
for his cowardship, ask Fabian.

FABIAN   A coward, a most devout coward, religious
in it!

SIR ANDREW   'Slid! I'll after him again and beat him.

SIR TOBY   Do, cuff him soundly, but never draw thy
sword.

SIR ANDREW   An I do not –   [*Exit*

FABIAN   Come, let's see the event.

SIR TOBY   I dare lay any money, 'twill be nothing yet. 410
                                    [*Exeunt*

3   Go to *Off with you!*

5   held out *kept up*

10   vent *utter; get rid of*

14   lubber *lout*
15   cockney *affected fop*
15–6   ungird . . . strangeness *abandon thy reserved behaviour*
16   vent *say*
18   foolish Greek *buffoon*

23   after . . . purchase *at a price equivalent to fourteen years' rent, i.e. at a high price. The price of land was usually the equivalent of twelve years' rent.*

28   your dagger *Perhaps Sebastian threatens Andrew with his dagger, or beats him with the handle of his dagger.*

144

ACT FOUR

Scene 1. *Enter* SEBASTIAN *and* FESTE

FESTE Will you make me believe that I am not sent for you?

SEBASTIAN Go to, go to, thou art a foolish fellow. Let me be clear of thee.

FESTE Well held out, i'faith. No: I do not know you; nor I am not sent to you by my lady, to bid you come speak with her; nor your name is not Master Cesario; nor this is not my nose, neither. Nothing that is so, is so.

SEBASTIAN I prithee, vent thy folly somewhere else; 10
thou know'st not me.

FESTE Vent my folly! He has heard that word of some great man, and now applies it to a fool. Vent my folly! I am afraid this great lubber the world will prove a cockney. I prithee now, ungird thy strangeness, and tell me what I shall vent to my lady? Shall I vent to her that thou art coming?

SEBASTIAN I prithee, foolish Greek, depart from me. There's money for thee; if you tarry longer, I shall give worse payment. 20

FESTE By my troth, thou hast an open hand! These wise men that give fools money get themselves a good report – after fourteen years' purchase.

Enter SIR ANDREW, TOBY, *and* FABIAN

SIR ANDREW Now, sir, have I met you again? There's for you!

He strikes SEBASTIAN

SEBASTIAN Why, there's for thee! And there!

He beats SIR ANDREW

And there! Are all the people mad?

SIR TOBY Hold, sir, or I'll throw your dagger o'er the house.

145

30   straight *at once*

34   action *law-suit. As Andrew struck first he can scarcely
            charge Sebastian with assault and battery!*

39   iron *Cant for 'sword'.*
            fleshed *blooded*

42   tempt *put to the test; incite (to hurt you)*

44   .   malapert *saucy*

51   Rudesby *ruffian, boor*

52   sway *rule*
53   uncivil *barbarous*
            extent *assault (legal term)*

56   botched up *clumsily contrived*

FESTE   This will I tell my lady straight. I would   30
    not be in some of your coats, for twopence.   [*Exit*
SIR TOBY   Come on, sir, hold!
SIR ANDREW   Nay, let him alone. I'll go another way to
    work with him. I'll have an action of battery against
    him, if there be any law in Illyria – though I struck
    him first, yet it's no matter for that.
SEBASTIAN   Let go thy hand!
SIR TOBY   Come, sir, I will not let you go. Come, my
    young soldier, put up your iron; you are well fleshed.
    Come on!   40
SEBASTIAN   I will be free from thee!
          He breaks free and draws his sword
                              What wouldst thou now?
          If thou dar'st tempt me further, draw thy sword.
SIR TOBY   What, what! Nay, then, I must have an
    ounce or two of this malapert blood from you.
                         He draws
                         Enter OLIVIA
OLIVIA   Hold, Toby! On thy life, I charge thee
                hold!
SIR TOBY   Madam!
OLIVIA   Will it be ever thus? Ungracious wretch,
          Fit for the mountains and the barbarous caves
          Where manners ne'er were preached, out of my
                sight!
          Be not offended, dear Cesario.   50
          Rudesby, be gone!
             [*Exeunt* SIR TOBY, SIR ANDREW *and* FABIAN
                              I prithee, gentle friend,
          Let thy fair wisdom, not thy passion, sway
          In this uncivil and unjust extent
          Against thy peace. Go with me to my house,
          And hear thou there how many fruitless pranks
          This ruffian hath botched up, that thou thereby
          Mayst smile at this. Thou shalt not choose but
                go;

58   deny *refuse*
     Beshrew *A plague upon (mild oath)*
59   started *roused (a hunting term), alarmed*
     heart *Quibbling on* hart, *and the conceit that lovers exchange hearts.*
60   relish *taste; quality.* 'What does this mean?'
61   Or . . . or *Either . . . or*
62   Lethe *The mythical river of forgetfulness.* 'Let delusive imagination continue to steep my mind in forgetfulness.'

ACT FOUR, scene 2

2   Sir Topas *The name of the ridiculous hero of Chaucer's* Rime of Sir Topas. *It may be significant that precious stones were thought to have healing powers; the* topaz *cured lunacy.*
3   curate *parish priest*
4   dissemble *disguise*

7   function *employment*

9   good housekeeper *solid citizen*
9–10   careful *watchful, painstaking*
10   competitors *confederates*

12   Bonos dies *Good day*
12–13   old . . . Prague *Feste's invention, to ridicule the scholarly use of 'authorities'.*
14   King Gorboduc *A legendary king of Britain.*

19   knave *lad. Often used in friendly familiarity of servants.*
20   [Within] *Throughout this scene Malvolio speaks from the* dark room *(III. 4. 143), off-stage. Does an invisible Malvolio appeal more strongly to our pity?*

148

Do not deny. Beshrew his soul for me!
He started one poor heart of mine, in thee.

SEBASTIAN   [*Aside*] What relish is in this? How runs
            the stream?   60
      Or I am mad, or else this is a dream.
      Let fancy still my sense in Lethe steep;
      If it be thus to dream, still let me sleep!

OLIVIA   Nay, come I prithee. Would thou'dst be
            ruled by me!

SEBASTIAN   Madam, I will.

OLIVIA   O, say so, and so be!

                                              [*Exeunt*

Scene 2. *Enter* MARIA *and* FESTE

MARIA   Nay, I prithee, put on this gown and this
      beard; make him believe thou art Sir Topas the
      curate. Do it quickly. I'll call Sir Toby the whilst.

                                              [*Exit*

FESTE   Well, I'll put it on and I will dissemble
      myself in't, and I would I were the first that ever
      dissembled in such a gown. I am not tall enough to
      become the function well, nor lean enough to be
      thought a good student. But to be said an honest man
      and a good housekeeper goes as fairly as to say a care-
      ful man and a great scholar. The competitors enter.   10
                Enter SIR TOBY *and* MARIA

SIR TOBY   Jove bless thee, Master Parson!

FESTE   *Bonos dies*, Sir Toby; for as the old hermit
      of Prague that never saw pen and ink very wittily said
      to a niece of King Gorboduc: that that is, is. So I,
      being Master Parson, am Master Parson; for what is
      'that' but 'that'? And 'is' but 'is'?

SIR TOBY   To him, Sir Topas.

FESTE   What ho, I say! Peace in this prison!

SIR TOBY   The knave counterfeits well; a good knave.

MALVOLIO   [*Within*] Who calls there?   20

25   hyperbolical *boisterous (addressing the fiend by which Malvolio is supposedly possessed)*

32   modest *moderate, mild*

34   house (*madman's*) *cell*

37   barricadoes *barricades*
        clerestories *upper windows*
38   lustrous *bright*
39   obstruction *shutting out of light*

44   Egyptians *Moses brought a thick darkness that lasted three days to plague the Egyptians: Exodus X. 21–23.*

47   abused *badly used*
48–9   constant question *logical discussion*

50   Pythagoras *Greek philosopher who expounded the theory of the transmigration of souls, i.e. that one soul could successively inhabit animals and men.*

53   happily *haply, perhaps; contentedly*

FESTE   Sir Topas the curate, who comes to visit
Malvolio the lunatic.

MALVOLIO   Sir Topas, Sir Topas, good Sir Topas, go
to my lady –

FESTE   Out, hyperbolical fiend, how vexest thou
this man! Talkest thou nothing but of ladies?

SIR TOBY   Well said, Master Parson.

MALVOLIO   Sir Topas, never was man thus wronged.
Good Sir Topas, do not think I am mad. They have
laid me here in hideous darkness –   30

FESTE   Fie, thou dishonest Satan! I call thee by
the most modest terms, for I am one of those gentle
ones that will use the devil himself with courtesy.
Sayst thou that house is dark?

MALVOLIO   As hell, Sir Topas.

FESTE   Why, it hath bay windows transparent as
barricadoes, and the clerestories toward the south-
north are as lustrous as ebony. And yet complainest
thou of obstruction!

MALVOLIO   I am not mad, Sir Topas. I say to you, this   40
house is dark.

FESTE   Madman, thou errest. I say there is no
darkness but ignorance, in which thou art more
puzzled than the Egyptians in their fog.

MALVOLIO   I say this house is as dark as ignorance,
though ignorance were as dark as hell. And I say
there was never man thus abused. I am no more mad
than you are – make the 'trial of it in any constant
question.

FESTE   What is the opinion of Pythagoras con-   50
cerning wildfowl?

MALVOLIO   That the soul of our grandam might
happily inhabit a bird.

FESTE   What think'st thou of his opinion?

MALVOLIO   I think nobly of the soul, and no way
approve his opinion.

FESTE   Fare thee well; remain thou still in dark-

59   allow . . . wits *acknowledge your sanity*
            woodcock *a proverbially foolish bird*

64   for all waters *ready for anything(?)*
65–6   Thou . . . not *Shakespeare probably made Feste disguise
            himself to help the audience.*

69   delivered *released*

72   upshot *conclusion*

73–80   Hey . . . another *Feste sings snatches of an old ballad.*

76   perdy (*French* par Dieu) *A mild oath.*

88–9   besides . . . wits *i.e. out of your mind. The five wits were
            the five faculties of the mind: common wit, imagina-
            tion, fantasy, estimation, memory.*

152

ness. Thou shalt hold th' opinion of Pythagoras ere I will allow of thy wits, and fear to kill a woodcock lest thou dispossess the soul of thy grandam. Fare thee well.   60

MALVOLIO   Sir Topas, Sir Topas!

SIR TOBY   My most exquisite Sir Topas!

FESTE   Nay, I am for all waters.

MARIA   Thou mightst have done this without thy beard and gown; he sees thee not.

SIR TOBY   To him in thine own voice, and bring me word how thou find'st him. I would we were well rid of this knavery. If he may be conveniently delivered, I would he were, for I am now so far in offence with   70 my niece that I cannot pursue with any safety this sport to the upshot. Come by and by to my chamber.

                          [*Exeunt* SIR TOBY *and* MARIA

FESTE [*Sings*]
    'Hey Robin, jolly Robin!
    Tell me how thy lady does –'

MALVOLIO   Fool!

FESTE [*Sings*]
    'My lady is unkind, perdy.'

MALVOLIO   Fool!

FESTE [*Sings*]
    'Alas, why is she so?'

MALVOLIO   Fool, I say!

FESTE [*Sings*]
    'She loves another –'   80
Who calls, ha?

MALVOLIO   Good fool, as ever thou wilt deserve well at my hand, help me to a candle, and pen, ink, and paper. As I am a gentleman, I will live to be thankful to thee for't.

FESTE   Master Malvolio?

MALVOLIO   Ay, good fool.

FESTE   Alas, sir, how fell you besides your five wits?

90   notoriously *outrageously*

94   propertied *used me as a mere property or object*

96   face *bully*
97   Advise you *Be careful*

100   bibble-babble *A pun on 'Bible babble'*.

103–4   God buy you *God be with you*

108   shent *scolded*

112   Well-a-day, that *Alas, if only*

124–31   I . . . devil *Here Feste may improvise a doggerel poem,
          and not sing. The last word (devil) affords a neat
          insult.*
124   anon *soon*

154

MALVOLIO   Fool, there was never man so notoriously   90
abused. I am as well in my wits, fool, as thou art.

FESTE   But as well? Then you are mad indeed, if
you be no better in your wits than a fool.

MALVOLIO   They have here propertied me; keep me
in darkness, send ministers to me – asses! – and do all
they can to face me out of my wits.

FESTE   Advise you what you say. The minister is
here. [*In the voice of Sir Topas*] Malvolio, Malvolio,
thy wits the heavens restore! Endeavour thyself to
sleep, and leave thy vain bibble-babble.   100

MALVOLIO   Sir Topas!

FESTE   Maintain no words with him, good fellow.
[*In his own voice*] Who, I, sir? Not I, sir! God buy
you, good Sir Topas! [*In the voice of Sir Topas*]
Marry, amen! [*In his own voice*] I will, sir, I will.

MALVOLIO   Fool! Fool! Fool, I say!

FESTE   Alas, sir, be patient. What say you sir? I
am shent for speaking to you.

MALVOLIO   Good fool, help me to some light and some
paper. I tell thee, I am as well in my wits as any man 110
in Illyria.

FESTE   Well-a-day, that you were, sir!

MALVOLIO   By this hand, I am! Good fool, some ink,
paper, and light; and convey what I will set down to
my lady. It shall advantage thee more than ever the
bearing of letter did.

FESTE   I will help you to't. But tell me true, are
you not mad indeed, or do you but counterfeit?

MALVOLIO   Believe me, I am not. I tell thee true.

FESTE   Nay, I'll ne'er believe a madman till I see 120
his brains. I will fetch you light, and paper, and ink.

MALVOLIO   Fool, I'll requite it in the highest degree.
I prithee, be gone.

FESTE [*Sings*]
        I am gone, sir, and anon, sir,
            I'll be with you again.

126 Vice *A stock character in Morality plays and interludes,*
     a companion of the Devil, whom Vice often attacked
     and drove off the stage with his dagger of lath
     (*wooden dagger*).

130 Pare *Cut. Apparently it was a traditional piece of stage*
     business to cut the devil's nails. Compare Henry V,
     IV. 4. 69 ff., '*Bardolph . . . had ten times more*
     valour than this roaring devil i'th'old play, that
     every one may pare his nails with a wooden dagger.'

ACT FOUR, scene 3

6   there . . . was *he had been there*
     credit *report*
7   range *traverse, roam*

9   sense *the evidence of my senses*

12   instance *precedent*
     discourse *reason, thought*

15   trust *conviction*

17   sway *rule*

18   Take . . . dispatch '*Take*' *goes with* '*affairs*', '*give*
     back' *with* '*dispatch*', *i.e. take a business in hand and*
     discharge it.
19   smooth *pleasant, mild*
21   deceivable *deceptive*

24   chantry by *nearby chapel*

156

In a trice, like to the old Vice,
    Your need to sustain.
Who with dagger of lath, in his rage and his
    wrath,
    Cries 'Ah ha!' to the devil;
Like a mad lad – 'Pare thy nails, dad!   130
    Adieu, goodman devil!'   [*Exit*

Scene 3. *Enter* SEBASTIAN

SEBASTIAN   This is the air, that is the glorious sun;
    This pearl she gave me, I do feel't and see't;
    And though 'tis wonder that enwraps me thus,
    Yet 'tis not madness. Where's Antonio, then?
    I could not find him at the Elephant.
    Yet there he was, and there I found this credit
    That he did range the town to seek me out.
    His counsel now might do me golden service.
    For though my soul disputes well with my sense
    That this may be some error, but no madness,   10
    Yet doth this accident and flood of fortune
    So far exceed all instance, all discourse,
    That I am ready to distrust mine eyes,
    And wrangle with my reason that persuades me
    To any other trust but that I am mad –
    Or else the lady's mad; yet if 'twere so,
    She could not sway her house, command her
        followers,
    Take and give back affairs and their dispatch,
    With such a smooth, discreet, and stable bearing
    As I perceive she does. There's something in't   20
    That is deceivable. But here the lady comes.
          Enter OLIVIA *and a* PRIEST
OLIVIA   Blame not this haste of mine. If you mean
      well,
    Now go with me and with this holy man
    Into the chantry by; there before him

26	**Plight . . . faith** *Troth-plighting in the presence of a witness was a contract as binding as marriage.*
27	**jealous** *anxious*
	doubtful *apprehensive*
29	**Whiles** *Until*
	to note *to be made public*
30	**What time** *At which time*
	our . . . keep *celebrate our marriage ceremony*
31	**birth** *(noble) rank*
35	**fairly note** *look favourably upon*

And underneath that consecrated roof
Plight me the full assurance of your faith,
That my most jealous and too doubtful soul
May live at peace. He shall conceal it
Whiles you are willing it shall come to note; What time we will our celebration keep   30
According to my birth. What do you say?

SEBASTIAN   I'll follow this good man, and go with you,
And having sworn truth, ever will be true.

OLIVIA   Then lead the way, good father, and heavens so shine
That they may fairly note this act of mine!

[Exeunt

ACT FIVE, scene 1

1   his *Malvolio's*

6–7   This . . . again *Manningham (see p. 21) wrote in his Diary that 'one Dr Bullen, the Queen's kinsman, had a dog which he doted on so much that the Queen, understanding of it, requested he would grant her one desire, and he should have whatsoever he would ask. She demanded his dog. He gave it, and "Now, Madame," quoth he, "you promised to give me my desire . . . I pray you, give me my dog again"' (26 March 1603).*

9   trappings *ornaments, i.e. bits and pieces*

20   abused *deceived*

20–1   conclusions . . . kisses *if conclusions may be compared to kisses (and if a girl's 'no, no, no, no!' means 'Yes, yes!')*

29   double-dealing *giving twice; duplicity*

32   grace *A pun on (a) the form of address to a duke; (b) kindness, generosity; (c) Orsino's share of divine grace, which should prevent his listening to ill counsel.*

160

ACT FIVE

Scene 1. *Enter* FESTE *and* FABIAN

FABIAN   Now, as thou lov'st me, let me see his letter.

FESTE   Good Master Fabian, grant me another request.

FABIAN   Anything!

FESTE   Do not desire to see this letter.

FABIAN   This is to give a dog, and in recompense desire my dog again.

Enter ORSINO, VIOLA, CURIO, *and* LORDS

ORSINO   Belong you to the Lady Olivia, friends?

FESTE   Ay, sir, we are some of her trappings.

ORSINO   I know thee well. How dost thou, my good   10
fellow?

FESTE   Truly, sir, the better for my foes, and the worse for my friends.

ORSINO   Just the contrary: the better for thy friends.

FFSTE   No, sir: the worse.

ORSINO   How can that be?

FESTE   Marry, sir, they praise me – and make an ass of me. Now my foes tell me plainly, I am an ass; so that by my foes, sir, I profit in the knowledge of myself, and by my friends I am abused. So that, con-   20
clusions to be as kisses, if your four negatives make your two affirmatives, why then, the worse for my friends and the better for my foes.

ORSINO   Why, this is excellent.

FESTE   By my troth, sir, no – though it please you to be one of my friends.

ORSINO   Thou shalt not be the worse for me: there's gold.

FESTE   But that it would be double-dealing, sir, I would you could make it another.   30

ORSINO   O, you give me ill counsel!

FESTE   Put your grace in your pocket, sir, for this once, and let your flesh and blood obey it.

ORSINO   Well, I will be so much a sinner to be a double-dealer; there's another.

FESTE   *Primo, secundo, tertio,* is a good play, and the old saying is, the third pays for all; the triplex, sir, is a good tripping measure; or the bells of Saint Bennet, sir, may put you in mind – one, two, three!

ORSINO   You can fool no more money out of me at   40 this throw. If you will let your lady know I am here to speak with her, and bring her along with you, it may awake my bounty further.

FESTE   Marry, sir, lullaby to your bounty till I come again. I go, sir, but I would not have you to think that my desire of having is the sin of covetousness. But as you say, sir, let your bounty take a nap – I will awake it anon.   [*Exit*

              Enter ANTONIO *and the* OFFICERS

VIOLA   Here comes the man, sir, that did rescue me.

ORSINO   That face of his I do remember well.   50
           Yet when I saw it last it was besmeared
           As black as Vulcan in the smoke of war.
           A baubling vessel was he captain of,
           For shallow draught and bulk unprizable,
           With which such scatheful grapple did he make
           With the most noble bottom of our fleet,
           That very envy and the tongue of loss
           Cried fame and honour on him. What's the matter?

FIRST OFFICER Orsino, this is that Antonio
           That took the *Phoenix,* and her fraught from Candy;   60
           And this is he that did the *Tiger* board
           When your young nephew Titus lost his leg.
           Here in the streets, desperate of shame and state,
           In private brabble did we apprehend him.

VIOLA   He did me kindness, sir, drew on my side,
           But in conclusion put strange speech upon me.
           I know not what 'twas, but distraction.

68   Notable *Notorious*

70   terms *circumstances*
         dear *grievous*

78   rude *turbulent, rough*
79   wrack *wrecked (ship or) person*

81   retention *power of retaining, reservation*
82   All . . . dedication *all devoted to his service*
83   pure *purely*

88   to . . . acquaintance *i.e. to pretend impudently not to know me*
89   a . . . thing *a person estranged from me by a separation of twenty years*
90   While . . . wink *In the time that it would take one to wink*
91   recommended *committed*

ORSINO   Notable pirate, thou salt-water thief,
        What foolish boldness brought thee to their
          mercies
        Whom thou, in terms so bloody and so dear,   70
        Hast made thine enemies?
ANTONIO   Orsino, noble sir,
        Be pleased that I shake off these names you give
          me.
        Antonio never yet was thief or pirate,
        Though, I confess, on base and ground enough,
        Orsino's enemy. A witchcraft drew me hither,
        That most ingrateful boy there by your side
        From the rude sea's enraged and foamy mouth
        Did I redeem; a wrack past hope he was.
        His life I gave him, and did thereto add   80
        My love without retention or restraint,
        All his in dedication. For his sake
        Did I expose myself – pure for his love –
        Into the danger of this adverse town;
        Drew to defend him when he was beset;
        Where, being apprehended, his false cunning –
        Not meaning to partake with me in danger –
        Taught him to face me out of his acquaintance,
        And grew a twenty years' removèd thing
        While one would wink; denied me mine own
          purse   90
        Which I had recommended to his use
        Not half an hour before.
VIOLA   How can this be?
ORSINO   When came he to this town?
ANTONIO   Today, my lord; and for three months
          before,
        No interim, not a minute's vacancy,
        Both day and night, did we keep company.
          Enter OLIVIA *and* ATTENDANTS
ORSINO   Here comes the Countess; now heaven
          walks on earth!

99   Three months *Other clues suggest that only a few days have passed since the twins arrived in Illyria.*

101   but that *save that which*

106   Good . . . lord *Either a polite request to Orsino to let Cesario speak first, or addressed to Cesario (lord = husband).*

109   fat and fulsome *gross and nauseating*

113   ingrate . . . unauspicious *ungrateful and unpropitious*

114   have *Plural attracted by* off'rings

116   become *i.e. that shall be fitting for him*

118   Egyptian thief *In the* Ethiopica *of Heliodorus, the English translation of which went through several editions before 1600, the bandit Thyamis intends to kill Chariclea, whom he loves, to prevent her from falling into the hands of his enemies.*

121   non-regardance *contempt*

        cast *cast off; reckon, calculate*

122   that *since*

123   screws *wrenches*

126   tender *hold*

166

But for thee, fellow – fellow, thy words are
   madness.
Three months this youth hath tended upon me.
But more of that anon. Take him aside. 100

OLIVIA   What would my lord – but that he may not
   have –
Wherein Olivia may seem serviceable?
Cesario, you do not keep promise with me.

VIOLA   Madam?

ORSINO   Gracious Olivia –

OLIVIA   What do you say, Cesario? [*To* ORSINO]
   Good my lord –

VIOLA   My lord would speak; my duty hushes me.

OLIVIA   If it be aught to the old tune, my lord,
It is as fat and fulsome to mine ear
As howling after music.

ORSINO   Still so cruel? 110

OLIVIA   Still so constant, lord.

ORSINO   What, to perverseness? You uncivil lady,
To whose ingrate and unauspicious altars
My soul the faithfull'st off'rings have breathed
   out
That e'er devotion tendered! What shall I do?

OLIVIA   Even what it please my lord, that shall
   become him.

ORSINO   Why should I not – had I the heart to do
   it –
Like to th'Egyptian thief at point of death
Kill what I love? – a savage jealousy
That sometime savours nobly! But hear me this: 120
Since you to non-regardance cast my faith,
And that I partly know the instrument
That screws me from my true place in your
   favour,
Live you the marble-breasted tyrant still.
But this your minion, whom I know you love,
And whom, by heaven, I swear, I tender dearly,

128   in . . . spite *to the vexation of his master*

132   jocund *cheerful*
           apt *willing, ready*
133   do you rest *bring you peace*

136   mores *i.e. comparisons*

139   Ay me *Woe to me, alas for me*
           detested *The word recalls Latin* detestari, *to curse, and*
              testis, *a witness (since Viola appealed to* witnesses
              above). Here detested = *odious or hated person;*
              accursed person.

145   sirrah *A contemptuous mode of address to a menial.*

147   strangle . . . propriety *i.e. deny your identity.* Propriety
              also suggests 'ownership.'

150   that *him (Orsino)*

Him will I tear out of that cruel eye
Where he sits crownèd in his master's spite.
Come, boy, with me, my thoughts are ripe in
    mischief.
I'll sacrifice the lamb that I do love   130
To spite a raven's heart within a dove.

VIOLA   And I, most jocund, apt, and willingly,
To do you rest, a thousand deaths would die.

OLIVIA   Where goes Cesario?

VIOLA   After him I love
More than I love these eyes, more than my life,
More by all mores than ere I shall love wife.
If I do feign, you witnesses above,
Punish my life for tainting of my love!

OLIVIA   Ay me, detested! How am I beguiled!

VIOLA   Who does beguile you? Who does do you
    wrong?   140

OLIVIA   Hast thou forgot thyself? Is it so long?
Call forth the holy father!   [*Exit an* ATTENDANT

ORSINO   Come, away!

OLIVIA   Whither, my lord? Cesario, husband, stay!

ORSINO   Husband?

OLIVIA   Ay, husband. Can he that deny?

ORSINO   Her husband, sirrah?

VIOLA   No, my lord, not I.

OLIVIA   Alas, it is the baseness of thy fear
That makes thee strangle thy propriety.
Fear not, Cesario, take thy fortunes up,
Be that thou know'st thou art, and then thou art
As great as that thou fear'st.

                  Enter the PRIEST

                    O, welcome, Father.   150
Father, I charge thee, by thy reverence,
Here to unfold – though lately we intended
To keep in darkness what occasion now
Reveals before 'tis ripe – what thou dost know
Hath newly passed between this youth and me.

PRIEST   A contract of eternal bond of love,
Confirmed by mutual joinder of your hands,
Attested by the holy close of lips,
Strengthened by interchangement of your rings,
And all the ceremony of this compact   160
Sealed in my function, by my testimony;
Since when, my watch hath told me, toward my
    grave
I have travelled but two hours.

ORSINO   O thou dissembling cub! What wilt thou be
When time hath sowed a grizzle on thy case?
Or will not else thy craft so quickly grow
That thine own trip shall be thine overthrow?
Farewell, and take her; but direct thy feet
Where thou and I henceforth may never meet.

VIOLA   My lord, I do protest –

OLIVIA   O, do not swear!   170
Hold little faith, though thou hast too much fear.

Enter SIR ANDREW

SIR ANDREW   For the love of God, a surgeon! Send one
presently to Sir Toby.

OLIVIA   What's the matter?

SIR ANDREW   'Has broke my head across, and has given
Sir Toby a bloody coxcomb too. For the love of God,
your help! I had rather than forty pound I were at
home.

OLIVIA   Who has done this, Sir Andrew?

SIR ANDREW   The Count's gentleman, one Cesario. We 180
took him for a coward, but he's the very devil in-
cardinate.

ORSINO   My gentleman, Cesario?

SIR ANDREW   'Od's lifelings, here he is! You broke my
head for nothing; and that that I did, I was set on to
do't by Sir Toby.

VIOLA   Why do you speak to me? I never hurt you.
You drew your sword upon me without cause,
But I bespake you fair, and hurt you not.

171

SIR ANDREW If a bloody coxcomb be a hurt, you have 190
    hurt me. I think you set nothing by a bloody cox-
    comb. Here comes Sir Toby halting, you shall hear
    more; but if he had not been in drink, he would have
    tickled you othergates than he did.

ORSINO   How now, gentleman? How is't with you?

SIR TOBY   That's all one; 'has hurt me, and there's
    th' end on't. [*To* FESTE] Sot, didst see Dick Surgeon,
    sot?

FESTE   O, he's drunk, Sir Toby, an hour agone.
    His eyes were set at eight i'th' morning.   200

SIR TOBY   Then he's a rogue and a passy-measures
    pavin. I hate a drunken rogue.

OLIVIA   Away with him! Who hath made this havoc
    with them?

SIR ANDREW I'll help you, Sir Toby, because we'll be
    dressed together.

SIR TOBY   Will you help? An asshead, and a cox-
    comb, and a knave – a thin-faced knave, a gull!

OLIVIA   Get him to bed, and let his hurt be looked
    to.   210

                [*Exeunt* SIR TOBY *and* SIR ANDREW,
                          helped by FESTE *and* FABIAN
                Enter SEBASTIAN

SEBASTIAN   I am sorry, madam, I have hurt your
                kinsman.
    But had it been the brother of my blood
    I must have done no less, with wit and safety.
    You throw a strange regard upon me; and by
                that
    I do perceive it hath offended you.
    Pardon me, sweet one, even for the vows
    We made each other but so late ago.

ORSINO   One face, one voice, one habit, and two
                persons!
    A natural perspective, that is and is not.

174

SEBASTIAN   Antonio! O, my dear Antonio!   220
              How have the hours racked and tortured me
              Since I have lost thee!
ANTONIO   Sebastian, are you?
SEBASTIAN   Fear'st thou that, Antonio?
ANTONIO   How have you made division of yourself?
              An apple cleft in two is not more twin
              Than these two creatures. Which is Sebastian?
OLIVIA   Most wonderful!
SEBASTIAN   Do I stand there? I never had a brother,
              Nor can there be that deity in my nature
              Of here and everywhere. I had a sister   230
              Whom the blind waves and surges have
                devoured.
              Of charity, what kin are you to me?
              What countryman? What name? What
                parentage?
VIOLA   Of Messaline. Sebastian was my father.
              Such a Sebastian was my brother too.
              So went he suited to his watery tomb.
              If spirits can assume both form and suit
              You come to fright us.
SEBASTIAN   A spirit I am indeed,
              But am in that dimension grossly clad
              Which from the womb I did participate.   240
              Were you a woman, as the rest goes even,
              I should my tears let fall upon your cheek
              And say, 'Thrice welcome, drownèd Viola'.
VIOLA   My father had a mole upon his brow.
SEBASTIAN   And so had mine.
VIOLA   And died that day when Viola from her
                birth
              Had numbered thirteen years.
SEBASTIAN   O, that record is lively in my soul.
              He finishèd indeed his mortal act
              That day that made my sister thirteen years.   250
VIOLA   If nothing lets to make us happy both

But this my masculine usurped attire,
Do not embrace me, till each circumstance
Of place, time, fortune, do cohere and jump
That I am Viola; which to confirm
I'll bring you to a captain in this town
Where lie my maiden weeds; by whose gentle
    help
I was preserved to serve this noble Count.
All the occurrence of my fortune since
Hath been between this lady and this lord.   260

SEBASTIAN   [*To* OLIVIA] So comes it, lady, you have
        been mistook.
But nature to her bias drew in that –
You would have been contracted to a maid.
Nor are you therein, by my life, deceived:
You are betrothed both to a maid and man.

ORSINO   Be not amazed; right noble is his blood.
If this be so, as yet the glass seems true,
I shall have share in this most happy wrack.
[*To* VIOLA] Boy, thou hast said to me a thousand
    times
Thou never shouldst love woman like to me.   270

VIOLA   And all those sayings will I overswear
And all those swearings keep as true in soul
As doth that orbèd continent the fire
That severs day from night.

ORSINO   Give me thy hand,
And let me see thee in thy woman's weeds.

VIOLA   The Captain that did bring me first on
        shore
Hath my maid's garments. He, upon some action,
Is now in durance at Malvolio's suit,
A gentleman and follower of my lady's.

OLIVIA   He shall enlarge him; fetch Malvolio
        hither.   280
And yet, alas, now I remember me,
They say, poor gentleman, he's much distract.

283   extracting *distracting; quibbling on* extract = *to draw
          out of (my thoughts)*

286–7   he . . . end *he keeps the devil at a distance*
287   'Has *He has*

289   epistles *letters; with a quibble on 'New Testament
          letters'. Apparently a reference to a liturgical con-
          troversy as to when the gospel for the day should be
          read, or delivered.*
290   gospels *gospels of the New Testament; good tidings*
          skills *matters*
293   delivers *reads (the words of)*

296   An *If*

298   vox *the appropriate voice*

301   perpend *pay attention*

316   delivered *released*

Enter FESTE *with a letter, and* FABIAN
A most extracting frenzy of mine own
From my remembrance clearly banished his.
[*To* FESTE] How does he, sirrah?

FESTE   Truly, madam, he holds Beelzebub at the
stave's end as well as a man in his case may do. 'Has
here writ a letter to you – I should have given't you
today morning. But as a madman's epistles are no
gospels, so it skills not much when they are delivered.   290

OLIVIA   Open't, and read it.

FESTE   Look, then, to be well edified when the
fool delivers the madman. [*He reads, in a madman's
voice*] By the Lord, madam –

OLIVIA   How now, art thou mad?

FESTE   No, madam; I do but read madness. An
your ladyship will have it as it ought to be, you must
allow *vox*.

OLIVIA   Prithee, read i'thy right wits.

FESTE   So I do, madonna; but to read his right   300
wits is to read thus. Therefore perpend, my princess,
and give ear.

OLIVIA   [*Seizing the letter and giving it to* FABIAN]
Read it you, sirrah.

FABIAN   [*Reads*] By the Lord, madam, you wrong me,
and the world shall know it. Though you have put me
into darkness and given your drunken cousin rule over
me, yet have I the benefit of my senses as well as your
ladyship. I have your own letter that induced me to the
semblance I put on; with the which I doubt not but to do
myself much right, or you much shame. Think of me as   310
you please, I leave my duty a little unthought-of, and
speak out of my injury. The madly-used Malvolio.

OLIVIA   Did he write this?

FESTE   Ay, madam.

ORSINO   This savours not much of distraction.

OLIVIA   See him delivered, Fabian, bring him
        hither.   [*Exit* FABIAN

320   proper *own*
321   apt *ready*

322   quits *releases from service*

327   A sister (*And you shall from this time be*) a sister (*to me*)
you . . . she *Perhaps Olivia turned away to speak to a*
servant, and now has to guess which twin is she.

330   notorious *outrageous*

334   from it *differently*
335   invention *composition*

337   in . . . honour *with a becoming regard for your reputa-*
tion
338   lights *marks*

341   lighter *lesser*

My lord, so please you, these things further
   thought on,
To think me as well a sister as a wife,
One day shall crown th'alliance on't, so please
   you,
Here at my house, and at my proper cost.   320

ORSINO   Madam, I am most apt t'embrace your
   offer.
   [*To* VIOLA] Your master quits you; and for your
   service done him
So much against the mettle of your sex,
So far beneath your soft and tender breeding,
And since you called me master for so long,
Here is my hand; you shall from this time be
Your master's mistress.

OLIVIA   A sister, you are she.
   Enter MALVOLIO *and* FABIAN

ORSINO   Is this the madman?

OLIVIA   Ay, my lord, this same. How now, Malvolio?

MALVOLIO Madam, you have done me wrong, notorious wrong!   330

OLIVIA   Have I, Malvolio? No!

MALVOLIO Lady, you have; pray you, peruse that
   letter.
You must not now deny it is your hand.
Write from it if you can, in hand or phrase,
Or say 'tis not your seal, not your invention;
You can say none of this. Well, grant it then,
And tell me in the modesty of honour,
Why you have given me such clear lights of
   favour?
Bade me come smiling and cross-gartered to you,
To put on yellow stockings, and to frown   340
Upon Sir Toby and the lighter people?
And, acting this in an obedient hope,
Why have you suffered me to be imprisoned,

182

Kept in a dark house, visited by the priest,
And made the most notorious geck and gull
That e'er invention played on? Tell me why?

OLIVIA   Alas, Malvolio, this is not my writing,
Though, I confess, much like the character.
But out of question 'tis Maria's hand.
And now I do bethink me, it was she   350
First told me thou wast mad; then cam'st in
    smiling,
And in such forms which here were presupposed
Upon thee in the letter. Prithee, be content.
This practice hath most shrewdly passed upon
    thee;
But when we know the grounds and authors of it,
Thou shalt be both the plaintiff and the judge
Of thine own cause.

FABIAN   Good madam, hear me speak;
And let no quarrel, nor no brawl to come,
Taint the condition of this present hour,
Which I have wondered at. In hope it shall not 360
Most freely I confess, myself and Toby
Set this device against Malvolio here,
Upon some stubborn and uncourteous parts
We had conceived against him. Maria writ
The letter at Sir Toby's great importance,
In recompense whereof, he hath married her.
How with a sportful malice it was followed
May rather pluck on laughter than revenge,
If that the injuries be justly weighed
That have on both sides passed.   370

OLIVIA   Alas, poor fool! How have they baffled
    thee!

FESTE   Why, 'Some are born great, some achieve
greatness, and some have greatness thrown upon
them.' I was one, sir, in this interlude, one Sir Topas,
sir – but that's all one. 'By the Lord, fool, I am not
mad!' But do you remember: 'Madam, why laugh

378   whirligig *spinning top*
          his *its*

381   notoriously *See* *p. 9.*

384   convents *Either 'summons us' or 'is convenient'.*
385   combination *treaty, alliance*

389   habits *clothes*
390   fancy's *love's*

391   When that I was *Some think that this is an old folk-song, others that Armin (who acted Feste) composed it, others that Shakespeare wrote it. I assume (p. 21) that, whether Shakespeare wrote or borrowed the song, the play steers towards the wind and the rain. Another quatrain, with the same refrain, occurs in King Lear, III. 2. The song may have been intended as the 'jig' (lively song, or song and dance) that followed after an Elizabethan play, though modern actors prefer to sing it wryly or pathetically.*
          and a *a*
393   toy *trifle*
401   swaggering *bullying, blustering*

405   tosspots *topers, hard drinkers*
          still had I *always had*

you at such a barren rascal, an you smile not he's
gagged'? And thus the whirligig of time brings in his
revenges.

MALVOLIO   I'll be revenged on the whole pack of you! 380
                                                    [*Exit*

OLIVIA   He hath been most notoriously abused.
ORSINO   Pursue him and entreat him to a peace.
      He hath not told us of the Captain yet.
      When that is known, and golden time convents,
      A solemn combination shall be made
      Of our dear souls. Meantime, sweet sister,
      We will not part from hence. Cesario, come;
      For so you shall be, while you are a man.
      But when in other habits you are seen –
      Orsino's mistress, and his fancy's queen! 390
                                    [*Exeunt all but* FESTE

FESTE [*Sings*]
            When that I was and a little tiny boy,
               With hey, ho, the wind and the rain,
            A foolish thing was but a toy,
                  For the rain it raineth every day.

                  But when I came to man's estate,
               With hey, ho, the wind and the rain,
            'Gainst knaves and thieves men shut their gate,
                  For the rain it raineth every day.

                  But when I came, alas, to wive,
               With hey, ho, the wind and the rain, 400
            By swaggering could I never thrive,
                  For the rain it raineth every day.

                  But when I came unto my beds,
               With hey, ho, the wind and the rain,
            With tosspots still had drunken heads,
                  For the rain it raineth every day.

                  A great while ago the world began,
               With hey, ho, the wind and the rain,
            But that's all one, our play is done,
                  And we'll strive to please you every day. [*Exit* 410

Shakespeare Interviews

devised, written and directed by Robert Tanitch

Four tapes, each of which contains a brief introduction to
one of Shakespeare's most popular plays, followed by a
searching interview with the main characters in the play.
The actions and motives of the characters, and the conflict
and drama of their relationships are revealed through the
interviewer's skilful questioning.

Shakespeare Interviews can be enjoyed both at a simple
and a sophisticated level. For the student coming to
Shakespeare for the first time, these tapes will be invaluable
in helping him to overcome the initial language barrier.
For the student of Shakespeare at CSE, O and A level who
is familiar with the play which he is studying, these tapes
offer a stimulating approach, and a springboard for new
ideas.

Characters interviewed:
Macbeth: Macbeth, Lady Macbeth
Julius Caesar: Brutus, Cassius, Julius Caesar, Mark Antony
Hamlet: Hamlet, Ophelia, Polonius, Claudius, Gertrude
Romeo and Juliet: Romeo, Juliet, Mercutio, Friar Lawrence,
the Nurse

Macbeth	open reel 333 15111 9	cassette 333 15373 1
Julius Caesar	open reel 333 15112 7	cassette 333 15375 8
Hamlet	open reel 333 15113 5	cassette 333 15376 6
Romeo and		
Juliet	open reel 333 15114 3	cassette 333 15377 4